Using the Internet to Investigate Math

Walter Sherwood

J. WESTON

WALCH
PUBLISHER

Portland, Maine

User's Guide
to
Walch Reproducible Books

As part of our general effort to provide educational materials that are as practical and economical as possible, we have designated this publication a "reproducible book." The designation means that purchase of the book includes purchase of the right to limited reproduction of all pages on which this symbol appears:

Here is the basic Walch policy: We grant to individual purchasers of this book the right to make sufficient copies of reproducible pages for use by all students of a single teacher. This permission is limited to a single teacher, and does not apply to entire schools or school systems, so institutions purchasing the book should pass the permission on to a single teacher. Copying of the book or its parts for resale is prohibited.

Any questions regarding this policy or requests to purchase further reproduction rights should be addressed to:

Permissions Editor
J. Weston Walch, Publisher
321 Valley Street • P. O. Box 658
Portland, Maine 04104-0658

1   2   3   4   5   6   7   8   9   10

ISBN 0-8251-3745-4

Copyright © 1998
J. Weston Walch, Publisher
P. O. Box 658 • Portland, Maine 04104-0658

Printed in the United States of America

Contents

About the Author

Walter Sherwood is an award-winning educator who has taught middle school and high school mathematics. He currently works as an educational consultant, trainer, and writer, working with teachers and administrators to improve student performance. He has special expertise in linking mathematics with technology and conducts a variety of workshops that help teachers bring math alive by using the Internet in their classrooms. Walter is also the author of *Using the Internet to Investigate Algebra, Real-Life Math: Algebra,* and *Real-Life Math: Decimals and Percents,* all of which are published by J. Weston Walch.

To the Teacher

Imagine, if you will, a classroom of students acting as general contractors who are busy preparing a bid for painting their classroom. At the moment, some of the students are measuring the length and width of a wall in order to figure out its area; other students have finished measuring the walls and are carefully performing calculations to determine how many gallons of paint they will need. Yet another group of students has just accessed the Internet and gone on-line to a Paint Estimator web site and entered their measurements. In a split second, the Paint Estimator displays how many gallons of paint they will need. The students then go to two other web sites and collect similar data. They use the information from the web sites to make comparisons with their own calculations. When that's done, they will hypothesize why differences exist. Throughout this hands-on, interactive lesson, students remain actively engaged, work together, and solve meaningful problems with real-world applications.

For some, a scenario like that may sound far-fetched—unless, of course, you are harnessing the power of the Internet in your classroom. The 22 ready-to-use lesson plans and student activities in this book will help you make learning math fun, and it will get students interested in doing math by using a tool they enjoy—the Internet.

Acceptable Use Policies

Most districts and schools have "Acceptable Use Policies." It would be best to check your school or district's policy prior to allowing students access to the Internet.

How to Use the Lessons and Activities

The lessons and student activities in this book are straightforward and easy to use. However, to get the most out of them, take a moment and read through the suggestions that follow.

Using the Internet

Using the lessons requires a basic understanding of how to use the Internet. As a minimum, you should be able to enter a web-page address, also referred to as a Universal Resource Locator (URL), and you should also be able to "bookmark," or save, the address of a web page so that you can visit it later. If you've never been on-line or can't do either of these two items, don't panic; in less than five minutes most of the students in your class will be able to show you how to accomplish these tasks. Learning to use the Internet takes some time but is well worth the effort.

Verifying Web Pages

Although the web pages used in the activities were verified prior to publication, web sites can come and go without explanation or warning. So, it's important to verify the web pages prior to using the lesson. This isn't difficult and will only take a couple of minutes. To verify a web site, simply go to that site and make sure it is functioning. It's easy to make a mistake entering an address, so if your first attempt to access a web page fails, make sure that you've entered the address correctly. If you have entered the web-page address correctly and the site still will not come up, wait a short while and try again. At times, a site becomes inaccessible and you just need to wait until it is functioning again. If you determine that a web site is no longer working, you can take a few simple steps to identify an alternate site. Details on how to do this are included in the section on "Conducting Searches."

Computer Access

Having limited access to computers does not preclude you from using the lessons. Most of the lessons are designed so that computer time is kept to a minimum. For example, students might visit a web page for a couple of minutes, gather the necessary information, and use it to make a calculation. If you have limited access to computers, have students rotate their use. If your school has only one computer with Internet access, have one or two students be responsible for gathering data for the lesson and sharing it with the class, or rotate groups of students as appropriate. Many schools are set up with computers in a central location, such as in a computer lab. If this is the case, complete the sections of the lesson that can be done in class without Internet access, and then use your lab time to gather the necessary information to continue or complete the lesson. Another consideration is to have students look up some of the data at home or in a library if they have Internet access there. Of course, another consideration is to lobby your principal for more computers with Internet access at your school.

Math Topics Covered

The lessons in the book are not listed in any particular order. However, it is recommended that you begin with the activity "Where in the World Wide Web?" This lesson will help students become familiar with finding their way around the Internet, and it will teach them how to use their web browser. Each lesson can be used either to support or to extend a math topic that you are working on in class, or the lessons can be used to introduce a new topic. Either way you choose to use them, the math topics that each lesson covers are shown in the correlation grid on page *viii*.

Multiple Learning Styles

Many of the lessons engage students in hands-on activities and address different learning styles. This will help promote a high level of student interest and learning in your classroom.

Organizing the Classroom

The lesson plans have suggestions on how to group students for the activities. Some of the lessons work best for individual student work, other lessons are more appropriate for students working in pairs, and some lessons work best for groups of students. The final decision on how to organize your students is left up to you.

Evaluation and Assessment

Because the activities are purposefully designed to be "open-ended," evaluation may be a challenge at first. To help you evaluate student responses, a generic scoring rubric is included (see Appendix). Use this rubric as a guide to evaluate the quality of the students' work. You may wish to tailor the scoring rubric to fit the individual activities, or you may choose to develop your own means of assessment. Where appropriate, selected answers are given.

Time Considerations

Since students' ability levels and schools' schedules vary greatly, time suggestions for the lessons are not given. Review the lessons and decide how many class periods would be appropriate. Many of the lessons can be shortened or extended depending on which parts of the activity are used.

Web Browser Software

The lessons in this book are not dependent on using any particular web browser software. However, a current version of your browser will ensure greatest benefit from each lesson.

Conducting Searches

Specific web sites to use with each lesson are provided, and as mentioned earlier, you should make it a practice to verify those web sites prior to using each lesson. If you find that a referenced web site is no longer valid, you will need to locate a substitute site.

If you aren't familiar with how to conduct a search on the Internet, now is a good time to learn. Go to the button on your browser that says "Search" and click on it. At any one of the "search engines" that comes up (such as Yahoo!®, Excite^SM, Infoseek^TM, etc.), enter your keywords (what you're trying to find). If you want to find a combination of words, put them in quotation marks. For instance, if the lesson requires statistics for baseball players, you might search for "baseball player statistics." The search results are returned according to how they match up with your keywords. Read the descriptions for the top ten or so web sites, and decide if it is what you are searching for. If you think the web site contains the information you need, visit it (by clicking on the highlighted text) and evaluate the contents. Be sure to bookmark the sites that you want to use. At first it might seem overwhelming, since so many web sites are returned, but you can narrow the list of choices by carefully selecting your search criteria. For instance, in the example above, if you were interested in statistics only for active players, you might get better results by searching for more specific information, such as "active baseball player statistics." Sometimes searching for that perfect web site takes a little work, but if you're persistent and thorough, you will find what you're looking for.

Stay in Touch

If you find alternate web sites that will work with the lessons, let us know by sending e-mail to us at:

editorial@mail.walch.com

Math Topics Correlation

	Problem Solving	Number Relationships	Determining Average	Unit Conversion	Measurement	Estimation	Algebraic Concepts	Mean, Median, Mode, and Range	Graphing	Collecting Data	Geometric Concepts	Ratio and Proportion	Using Percents	Probability	Frequency Tables	Scientific Notation	Finding Area	Statistics	Analyzing Data	Equivalency	Metric Units	Interpreting Data
Where in the World Wide Web?	X	X							X	X									X			
One Step at a Time	X	X		X								X										
Buying Your First Car	X				X	X	X			X									X	X		
Got a Problem?	X									X					X				X			
Target Heart Rate	X							X	X	X			X						X	X		X
Working for a Living	X				X					X			X									
Road Trip	X		X			X				X												
Counting Heads	X	X			X							X			X							X
Games, Games, and More Games	X		X		X								X									X
Paint the Classroom	X			X	X		X				X		X				X					
Carpet the Classroom	X			X	X		X				X		X				X					
Measuring Your Fitness Level	X				X			X	X	X	X		X						X			X
What to Do with All Our Garbage?	X			X	X			X	X	X			X	X								
Counting Calories	X	X	X		X	X													X			
Burning Calories	X				X							X							X			
Cooking in Metric	X			X	X																X	
Coin Toss	X	X												X					X			
Dice Roll	X	X												X	X				X			
How Many People Have Ever Lived?	X				X		X						X			X			X	X	X	X
Batter up!	X	X							X										X	X	X	X
Chill Out	X		X		X				X	X									X	X		
The Heat Is On	X		X		X				X	X									X	X		

Where in the World Wide Web?

Overview:

In this activity students learn how to navigate the Internet by searching for information and facts. Then they use the information they found to solve math problems.

Learning Objectives:

- Locate facts and information on the Internet.
- Solve math problems with the information and facts found on the Internet.
- Learn basic search techniques.
- Become familiar with the capabilities of the web browser software being used.

Web Sites:

For this activity, specific web sites are not given.

Materials:

Computer with Internet access; calculator; graph paper

Suggestions:

1. Students should work individually when searching for the information so that they become familiar with how to use the Internet and their web browser software. However, you may decide to have them work in pairs or in groups to solve the problems.

2. Students will find the information they need to solve the problems at many different web sites. This being the case, it is important that students carefully list the web sites where they find their information.

3. To build excitement and motivation for the activity, you may want to have students compete to see who can locate the information and solve the problems the most quickly and accurately.

Selected Answers:

Answers will vary depending on where students find their information. Below are some possible web sites and answers for the problems.

Problem One:

Top 50 All-Time Grossing Movies
http://movieweb.com/movie/alltime.html

http://www.washingtonpost.com/wp-srv/style/daily/movies/100million/article.htm

1. Titanic, $601,000,000
2. Star Wars, $460,000,000
3. E.T., $407,000,000
4. Jurassic Park, $357,000,000
5. Forrest Gump, $327,000,000
Total Gross: 2.15×10^9

Problem Two:

McDonald's Nutritional Information
http://www.mcdonalds.com/food/nutrition/index.html

Wendy's Nutritional Information
http://www.wendys.com/the_menu/nut_frame.html

Burger King Nutritional Information
http://www.burgerking.com/nutrition.htm

McDonald's Quarter Pounder with cheese: 530 calories, 30 grams of fat.

Wendy's single cheeseburger: 490 calories, 25 grams of fat.

Burger King Whopper with cheese: 730 calories, 46 grams of fat.

Problem Three

Ford Expedition
http://www.edmunds.com/newtrucks

Chevrolet Suburban
http://www.edmunds.com/newtrucks

Suburban: 219.5 inches long, 7 Suburbans = 1536.5 inches total length;
Expedition: 204.6 inches long, 8 Expeditions = 1636.8 inches total length;
8 Expeditions are 100.3 inches longer than 7 Suburbans.

Problem Four:

List of week's TV ratings
http://www.usatoday.com/life/enter/tv/letindex.htm

1. Common choices are bar and line graphs
2. TV show names
3. Either number of homes or ratings points
4. Homes (intervals of about 5 million); ratings (intervals of about 1)

Problem Five:

Gap
http://www.gap.com/onlinestore/gap

Answers will vary depending upon types of jeans and shirts selected.

Extensions:

1. If your students are already skilled at navigating the Internet, you may want to have a contest to see who can find the most web sites that would provide the necessary information to solve the problems.

2. After students complete the activity, have them write a similar problem that uses information from the Internet to solve a math problem.

Where in the World Wide Web?

Trying to find information or a specific fact from the more than 40 million Internet web sites can be quite a challenge—but a challenge you are well able to meet. In this activity you will search for specific information or facts, then use that information to solve problems. The good news, of course, is that by the end of this lesson you will be an Internet expert.

Problem One

1. Find the five highest-grossing movies of all time, and list the total amount they grossed in the table below. After you list the movies and amounts, add the total earnings together. Write that amount in scientific notation.

Title	Gross (Round to Nearest 10 Million)
1.	
2.	
3.	
4.	
5.	

Gross amount for all five movies (scientific notation): _____

List the web site address where you found your information:

_____

Problem Two

Find out how many calories and grams of fat are in a McDonald's Quarter Pounder with cheese, Wendy's single cheeseburger with everything, and a Burger King Whopper with cheese. List the amounts in the table on the next page, then answer the three questions following the table.

(continued)

Where in the World Wide Web? *(continued)*

Name	Calories	Grams of Fat
McDonald's Quarter Pounder with cheese		
Wendy's single cheeseburger		
Burger King Whopper with cheese		

1. List the hamburgers in order from least to greatest according to their number of calories. Include appropriate inequality symbols.

2. List the hamburgers in order from least to greatest according to their number of fat grams. Include appropriate inequality symbols.

3. List the web site addresses where you found your information:

   McDonald's: _____

   Wendy's: _____

   Burger King: _____

Problem Three

Find an informational web page for each truck listed below. Then list the web page addresses and answer the questions that follow.

Chevrolet Suburban C2500 2WD: _____

Ford Expedition XLT 2WD: _____

1. If you lined up seven Suburbans end to end next to eight Expeditions end to end, which set of trucks would stretch farther and by how much?

(continued)

Where in the World Wide Web? *(continued)*

Length of one Chevrolet Suburban: _____   Length of seven Suburbans: _____

Length of one Ford Expedition: _____   Length of eight Expeditions: _____

The _____ would stretch farther by _____ feet.

2. Suppose you had a box shaped like a rectangular prism which measured 10 feet by 3 feet by 4 feet. Would you be able to fit this box into both vehicles? Explain.

Problem Four

Find a web site that lists the current week's TV-show rankings. On a separate sheet of paper, use that information to draw a graph comparing the top five shows. Then answer the questions that follow.

Web site address: _____

1. What type of graph did you make?_____

2. How did you label the x-axis (horizontal axis)? _____

3. How did you label the y-axis (vertical axis)? _____

4. What intervals did you choose for the y-axis? _____

Problem Five

Suppose your long-lost Great Aunt Zelda just sent you a long overdue birthday present of $200 cash. However, she made two conditions: You have to buy clothes, and you have to buy them at the Gap. Find the Gap web site and then answer the questions that follow.

Gap web site address: _____

1. If you bought two pairs of jeans, how much money would you have left to buy shirts?

    _____

2. If you bought three shirts, how many pairs of jeans could you then buy?

    _____

3. If you used the entire $200 on just jeans and shirts, what is the maximum number of each item you could buy so that you ended up with an equal number of jeans and shirts?

    _____

One Step at a Time

Overview:

In this activity students will organize a charity fundraiser using information from the Internet.

Learning Objectives:

- Organize data in charts.
- Measure the number of steps and the time it takes to go 20 feet.
- Calculate the number of steps to go a mile.
- Calculate the number of steps it will take to walk between cities.
- Evaluate the fundraising plan and make revisions as necessary.

Web Sites:

Map of United States
http://www.plasma.nationalgeographic.com/mapmachine/facts_fs.html

Distance between Cities
http://www.indo.com/distance

Conversion Factor Table
http://www.wctc.net/~wallin/convert

Materials:

Computer with Internet access; calculators; tape measure or yardstick; stopwatch; masking tape; poster paper

Suggestions:

1. Have students work in groups of three or four for this activity.

2. Students will have a lot of questions about which cities are okay to choose; any city on or near either coast will work.

3. Help students recognize that the distances between the cities are measured in straight lines; you may want to have students investigate adding additional miles to their routes to account for indirect routes. To do this, students may find it useful to select stopping points and add the distances that way.

4. Prior to the "Lots of steps" section, have students mark off 20 feet using masking tape and count how many steps it takes them to cover that distance.

5. Students will need to decide how they will use their data. Some may want to use the fastest times and least number of steps, some groups will want to find the mean, and others will select the slowest times or most steps. Regardless of which method they choose, ensure that they are able to support their choice.

Selected Answers:

Answers will vary depending on the cities students choose.

Extensions:

Have students figure out how many "walking days" each route would take. A "walking day" is the total number of hours you could expect to walk in a day.

Name _____   Date _____

One Step at a Time

Suppose you and a group of your friends are interested in raising money for a charity. You decide that a good way to do this is to organize a walk from the East Coast of the United States to the West Coast of the United States. To raise money, you plan on having sponsors make a pledge for each step you take. Follow the "steps" below to plan the fundraising event.

Find Your Way

First, decide on the cities you will start from and the cities you want to end up in. Then figure out how far you will have to walk. Visit the web site below and choose three different starting cities on the East Coast and three different cities to end up in on the West Coast. List them below.

Map of United States
http://www.plasma.nationalgeographic.com/mapmachine/facts_fs.html

East Coast Cities: West Coast Cities:

_____   _____

_____   _____

_____   _____

1. If you can start in any one of the three cities you selected on the East Coast and end up in any one of the three cities on the West Coast, how many different routes are possible? Explain.

   _____

   _____

   _____

2. For five of the possible routes, find out how far (in miles) the cities are apart. You can do this by visiting the web site below. Fill in the chart on the next page to help you organize your data.

Distance between Cities
http://www.indo.com/distance

(continued)

7   *Using the Internet to Investigate Math*

One Step at a Time *(continued)*

Starting City	Ending City	Distance (Miles)

Lots of Steps

Figure out how many steps it is going to take you to walk from coast to coast. For each group member, find out how many steps it takes to go 20 feet. Write the information in the table below.

Name	Number of Steps

1. Figure out the number of steps to go 20 feet that you will use for the group. _____

2. To calculate how many steps you will take on each route, you will need to know how many feet are in a mile. To find this information use the web page below. Once you know how many feet are in a mile, set up a proportion and solve for the number of steps you will need to go one mile.

Conversion Factor Table
http://www.wctc.net/~wallin/convert

Number of feet in one mile: _____

Number of steps in one mile: _____

(continued)

One Step at a Time *(continued)*

3. Now that you know how many steps you take in one mile and the number of miles between cities, you can find the total number of steps for each route. Select your three favorite routes. Calculate the total number of steps for each.

Route	Number of Steps

Raising Money

1. If you asked sponsors to pledge one cent per step, how much money would they be contributing for each of the three routes?

Route	Amount of Money Raised

2. After reviewing your information, your group decides that you can't expect people to pledge that much. You decide that a more realistic amount might be about $100 for the whole trip. Figure out how far you would have to go to raise $100 at one cent per step. Then go back to one of the web sites in question 1 and, starting in your own city, find three possible cities to end up in for that distance. When you have finished planning, design a flyer or brochure to advertise the fundraising event.

Buying Your First Car

Overview:

In this activity students will use the Internet to research and select three different used car models to consider purchasing. They will also compare the cars' "book value" with the actual costs found in newspapers around the country.

Learning Objectives:

- Calculate mean, median, mode, and range.
- Create a box and whisker plot.
- Calculate monthly payments and compare those amounts to loan payment calculators on the Internet.

Web Sites:

Edmunds
http://www.edmunds.com

Microsoft CarPoint
http://carpoint.msn.com

Kelly Blue Book
http://www.kbb.com

Newspapers
http://www.central.edu/Library/etexts.htm

Used Auto Loans by State
http://www.bankrate.com/edm/default.asp

Car Loan Calculator
http://www.edmunds.com/edweb/loan/calculator.html

Materials:

Computer with Internet access; calculator

Suggestions:

1. This activity works best for individual students, but it can also be used with pairs of students.
2. Review with students why used cars that are the same make, model, and year might differ in cost.
3. Students should visit at least 10 different newspapers; some students may need help identifying the "major" newspapers for each city.
4. Review with students how to construct a box and whisker plot.
5. Review terms such as annual percentage rate, principal, balance, and other words associated with loans.

Selected Answers:

Answers will vary depending on make, model, and year of cars selected.

Extensions:

Use a graphing calculator or spreadsheet for the statistical analysis portion of the lesson.

Buying Your First Car

Buying a car is a big decision. There are a lot of factors to consider: cost, make, model, year, loan amount, monthly payments, maintenance costs, and operating costs, to name a few. It sounds complicated, but if you attack the problem with an organized plan, you will be able to make a well-informed decision. Follow the steps below, and you will be well on your way to being ready to buy your first car.

Choose Your Car

Many young people start out by buying a used car, so for this activity you will consider only used cars. Some of you may already have a specific make, model, and year picked out, but for those of you who are not sure what kind of car you want, visit one of the web sites below and select at least three different used cars.

Edmunds
http://www.edmunds.com

Microsoft CarPoint
http://carpoint.msn.com

The three cars I selected are (list make, model, and year):

_____   _____   _____

Book Value

When you are buying a car, it is important to know how much the car *should* cost. Most people refer to this cost as "book value." To find out how much the cars you selected should cost, you can consult a buying guide, such as *Edmunds* or the *Kelly Blue Book*. Go to the web pages below. Find out the book values for the cars you selected. List the book values in the table below.

Edmunds
http://www.edmunds.com

Kelly Blue Book
http://www.kbb.com

Car Make, Model, and Year	*Edmunds* Price	*Kelly Blue Book* Price

(continued)

Name _____   Date _____

Buying Your First Car *(continued)*

Actual Cost

Knowing the book value for your cars is only half the story. You also need to find out how much you can actually buy the cars for. To do this, use the classified ads in newspapers around the country. Locate newspapers at the web site below. Locate as many of the cars you selected as you can in these ads. You must get information from at least 10 different newspapers. Find as many cars of the same model and year as you can in each paper. Try to find 20 prices for each of the three cars you are considering. List the car prices and the names of the newspapers in the table labeled "Car Prices" at the end of this handout.

Newspapers
http://www.central.edu/Library/etexts.htm

Evaluate the Cost

1. Use the price data you collected for each car to find the mean, median, mode, and range for the prices of each vehicle. List the amounts below.

	1	2	3
Car Name			
Mean Price			
Median Price			
Mode Price			
Price Range			

2. How do the actual selling prices you found compare with the car's book value? Explain.

   _____

   _____

3. On a separate sheet of paper, organize the price data you collected and create a box and whisker plot for the prices of one of the cars.

Car Loans

Most people need to borrow money to buy a car. Before you take out a loan, you need to know the annual percentage rate and the terms of the loan. Visit at least five banks or credit unions on the Internet. Find out their used car loan rates. To find a bank or credit union, you can search for a specific institution, make a more generic search for "banks" or "credit

(continued)

Buying Your First Car *(continued)*

unions," or use the web site below to find lending institutions in your state. Record your results in the table.

Used Car Loans by State
http://www.bankrate.com/edm/default.asp

Bank or Credit Union	Annual Percentage Rate (APR)	Number of Months

Using the information you collected from the banks and credit unions, find your monthly loan payments. To find your monthly loan amounts, go to the web site listed below. Assume that you will put no money down.

Car Loan Calculator
http://www.edmunds.com/edweb/loan/calculator.html

Name of Car	Loan Amount	Terms	Monthly Payment

2. Go back to the monthly loan calculator. For each loan, decrease the number of years by one. How does the decrease in the number of years affect the amount of the monthly loan payments?

_____

3. Go back to the monthly loan calculator. Increase the annual percentage rate by one percentage point. How does the increase in the annual percentage rate affect the amount of the monthly loan payments?

_____

4. Explain which of the cars is the best deal.

_____

(continued)

Buying Your First Car *(continued)*

CAR PRICES

Car Name:		Car Name:		Car Name:	
Price	Newspaper	Price	Newspaper	Price	Newspaper

Got a Problem?

Overview:

In this lesson students learn about effective problem-solving strategies, then apply what they have learned to solve some problems.

Learning Objectives:

- Identify the four basic steps in the problem-solving method presented.
- Identify the eight basic categories of problem-solving strategies.
- Solve problems using these strategies.
- Identify which strategies are used in solving problems.
- Construct a frequency table on problem-solving strategies.

Web Sites:

MATHCOUNTS Problem Solving Strategies
http://mathcounts.org/problems/strategies.html

Math Puzzles
http://www.eduplace.com/math/brain
or
http://www.thewizardofodds.com/math

Materials:

Computer with Internet access; calculator

Suggestions:

1. At first, students should work individually to investigate the problem-solving strategies web page. You may then choose to have them work in pairs or small groups to solve the problems and collect the data.

2. There are hundreds of sites with problems available on the Internet; the web site given is just a place to start. Depending on the needs of your students, you may select other sites or use other materials.

3. Some students will need a review on how to construct a frequency table.

4. Collect the number of times individual students used each strategy and write that information on an overhead or board so students are able to analyze the data for the entire class.

Selected Answers:

Problem-Solving Strategies: 1. Find out, Choose a strategy, Solve it, and Look back, 2. Make a Model (M), Make a Table (T), Guess, Check and Revise (G), Simplify (S), Eliminate (E), Look for Patterns (P), Compute or Simplify (C), Use a Formula (F).

Extensions:

Have students construct a poster for the classroom or their notebooks showing the four steps of the problem-solving method presented. They can also construct a poster showing the eight basic categories of problem-solving strategies.

Other Problem-Solving Web Sites:

Brain Teasers
http://www.hmco.com/school/math/brain/

Mike's Page of Math Problems
http://www.charm.net/~shack/math/

Got a Problem?

Does the thought of doing a word problem make you want to cry? If so, then you might want to think about improving your problem-solving skills. The best problem solvers use carefully selected strategies to solve problems. The good news is that you, too, can use those same problem-solving strategies. To become a better problem solver, start working through the activity below.

Problem-Solving Strategies

Good problem solvers have a plan and use proven problem-solving strategies. But what makes a good plan, and what are those proven strategies? Go to the MATHCOUNTS Problem-Solving Strategies web page and read about good problem-solving strategies. When you finish reading the article, answer the questions that follow.

MATHCOUNTS Problem-Solving Strategies
http://mathcounts.org/problems/strategies.html

1. List the four basic steps of the problem-solving method presented.

     _____   _____

     _____   _____

2. List the eight basic categories of problem-solving strategies below. After each category, write a brief description in your own words that explains how that strategy is used.

    1) _____ : _____

       _____

    2) _____ : _____

       _____

    3) _____ : _____

       _____

    4) _____ : _____

       _____

    5) _____ : _____

       _____

(continued)

Got a Problem? *(continued)*

6) _____ : _____

   _____

7) _____ : _____

   _____

8) _____ : _____

   _____

Solve Some Problems

Go to the web pages below and solve at least eight problems. Write down the names of the problems you solved and which of the eight strategies you used to solve them. Remember, concentrate on using good problem-solving strategies.

Math Puzzles
http://www.thewizardofodds.com/math
or
http://www.eduplace.com/math/brain

Problem Name	Strategy

(continued)

Got a Problem? *(continued)*

Findings

Look over the problems you solved. Construct a frequency table that shows the number of times you used each strategy. Write down your results and give them to your teacher. Then collect the same information from the rest of the class. Enter that information in the table below.

PROBLEM-SOLVING STRATEGIES USED

Strategies:	Make a Model (M)	Make a Table (T)	Guess, Check and Revise (G)	Simplify (S)	Eliminate (E)	Look for Patterns (P)	Compute or Simplify (C)	Use a Formula (F)
No. of Times You Used Strategy								
Frequency								
No. of Times Class Used Strategy								

1. Which two problem-solving strategies were used most often by the class. Why?

   _____

   _____

   _____

   _____

2. Suppose a new student enrolled in your class and had missed this activity. If the teacher asked you to write a brief summary explaining the problem-solving procedure and the eight categories of problem-solving strategies, what would you write?

   _____

   _____

   _____

   _____

Target Heart Rate

Overview:

In this activity students will learn how to use their pulse rates to determine their levels of fitness.

Learning Objectives:

- Learn how to measure pulse rates.
- Evaluate level of fitness using pulse rate.
- Determine target heart rate.
- Collect and analyze data for the class.

Web Sites:

Understanding Your Target Heart Rate
http://www.goodhealth.com/livewell/sport/library/heartrate.html

Target Heart Rate Calculator
http://www.nmia.com/~jkelly/java/target.html

Materials:

Computer with Internet access; tape measure; stopwatch or timer; calculator

Suggestions:

1. This activity should be done in pairs or in small groups.
2. Ensure that students have been resting or sitting still for a short while prior to taking their resting pulse rates. You may choose to have them take their pulses at the same time over an extended period of time and then average those results.
3. Record the pulse rates on the board or overhead as the students report them to you.
4. Simple activities, such as jumping jacks or walking up a flight of steps, work best for obtaining active pulse rates.

Selected Answers:

Answers will vary depending on pulse rates.

Extensions:

Have students solve problems such as the following: How many times does your heart beat in a hour, day, year, lifetime?

Target Heart Rate

How fit are you? Sounds like an easy question, but how can you accurately measure your fitness level? One way is by measuring your pulse rate and watching how it changes as you exercise. Begin the investigation below to find out how fit you are.

Resting Pulse

Measuring your resting pulse rate is one of the most common ways to determine your fitness level. Go to the web page below and learn how to take your pulse.

Understanding Your Target Heart Rate
http://www.goodhealth.com/livewell/sport/library/heartrate.html

1. Follow the directions on the Understanding Your Heart Rate web page. Take your resting pulse rate three different times. Instead of doing it at home when you wake up, as suggested on the web page, you will have to do it in class. Before you take your pulse, make sure you have been sitting quietly and still for a short while. After you have taken your resting pulse three times, calculate your average resting pulse rate. Write it down and give it to your teacher.

   Resting Pulse Rate:

   1) _____   2) _____   3) _____

   Average Resting Pulse Rate: _____

2. Why is it important to know your resting pulse rate?

   _____

   _____

3. Fill in the table with the average resting pulse rates for each student in the class. Then calculate the mean, median, mode, and range for the resting pulse rates for the class.

CLASS'S RESTING PULSE RATES

Mean: _____   Median: _____

Mode: _____   Range: _____

(continued)

     Using the Internet to Investigate Math

Target Heart Rate *(continued)*

4. Look over the class mean and your resting pulse rate average. Is your average resting pulse rate greater than, less than, or equal to (>,<,=) the class average? Write an inequality that shows this relationship.

   _____

5. Predict how the median pulse rate for the class would change if you threw out the highest and lowest individual pulse rate averages.

   _____

   _____

Target Heart Rate

1. Visit the Understanding Your Target Heart Rate web page again, and list the percentages for each target heart rate zone—Beginner, Average, and High. After you have listed the percentage ranges, write down the Karvonen Formula, which is used to determine your target heart zone.

   Beginner or low fitness level   From _____ % to _____%

   Average fitness level   From _____ % to _____%

   High fitness level   From _____ % to _____%

   Karvonen Formula: _____

   _____

2. Using the Karvonen Formula and your average resting pulse rate, calculate your target heart rate range for each level of fitness. Display your results below. Answers should be given as a range.

   Beginner or low fitness level range: _____

   Average fitness level range: _____

   High fitness level range: _____

3. The web site below calculates your target heart rate zone. Visit the site to verify your answers to question 2.

   Target Heart Rate Calculator
   http://www.nmia.com/~jkelly/java/target.html

   (continued)

Target Heart Rate *(continued)*

4. Were your calculations for question 2 accurate according to the target heart calculator on the web page? Explain.

   _____

   _____

5. On a separate sheet of paper, construct a graph that shows the different pulse rate ranges and fitness level percentage ranges.

Active Pulse Rate

Find out how your pulse rate changes as you exercise.

1. In your group, agree on a short physical activity that each group member will do. Complete the activity three times. Measure your pulse immediately following each time. Record your pulse rate in the space below. When you have done the activity three times, calculate your average active pulse rate. Write it down and give it to your teacher.

   Active Pulse Rates:

   1) _____   2) _____   3) _____

   Average Active Pulse Rate: _____

2. Fill in the table with the average active pulse rates for each student in the class. Then calculate the mean, median, mode, and range for the active pulse rates for the class.

CLASS'S ACTIVE PULSE RATES

   Mean: _____   Median: _____

   Mode: _____   Range: _____

3. How can you use what you have learned about pulse rates to improve your fitness level?

   _____

   _____

   _____

Working for a Living

Overview:

In this lesson students use the Internet to help them make a budget.

Learning Objectives:

- Select an occupation and determine the salary for that occupation.
- Use the salary as a basis for calculating percentages.
- Determine levels of expenses in given categories.
- Construct a budget in which expenses are less than income.

Web Sites:

College Board Career Search
http://cbweb9p.collegeboard.org/career/bin/career.pl

Apartments on Line
http://www.rent.net

CarPoint
http://carpoint.msn.com

Edmunds
http://www.edmunds.com

Car Loan Calculator
http://www.edmunds.com/edweb/loan/calculator.html

Student Loan Calculator
http://www.studentloan.com/slcsite/fr_tools.htm

Materials:

Computer with Internet access; calculator

Suggestions:

1. This activity is intended to be completed by individual students. However, it can also be done by a pair of students who make individual budgets but assume they are roommates sharing whatever expenses they can.

2. Students may need help determining income levels, since the salary amounts are listed in many different ways.

3. Demonstrate for the class how to calculate the percent of a number prior to having students work through the lesson.

4. Many students will need assistance determining appropriate amounts for such items as rent, food, etc.

5. Most problems with the budget occur because students select cars that are too expensive. Have them consider a less expensive car.

Selected Answers:

Answers will vary depending on chosen occupation and differences in expense amounts.

Extensions:

1. Categorize the expenses into five or six topics and have students construct a pie chart.

2. Have students explore more than one possible occupation.

3. Have students use a spreadsheet program to construct their budgets.

Name _____   Date _____

Working for a Living

Have you ever asked your parents to buy you something and been told "we can't afford it?" Well, that's because most people live on a budget. A budget is a listing of all your money (income) and all the things you spend it on (expenses). Sounds like a simple idea, but it can be quite a challenge to make a realistic budget, and an even bigger challenge to stick with it. But it's important to learn how to make and use a budget, since you too will soon have to live by one.

Income

1. A budget starts with knowing how much money you bring in each month. How much you bring in each month depends on your occupation. What do you hope to do after you finish school? Go to the web site below. Follow the pointers to your intended occupation. Find the median annual starting salary for your chosen field and list that amount below. You will use this amount to figure out your monthly net income (income after taxes).

   College Board Career Search
   http://cbweb9p.collegeboard.org/career/bin/career.pl

   Occupation: _____

   Median annual starting salary: _____

   Gross monthly income: _____

   Monthly net income after taxes (use a tax rate between 15% and 20%): _____
   Enter this amount on the Budget Worksheet in the space marked Monthly Net Income.

Expenses

Expenses are basically the opposite of income—money you spend on the things you need or want. There are many different things to choose from when deciding how to spend your money. However, some basic categories of expenses are necessities. We will focus on those. Listed below are 11 different expense categories. As you figure out each amount, enter that figure in your budget worksheet.

1. ***Housing***. Housing is usually the single largest expense in your budget. Go to the web site below and find an apartment that is right for you. List the amount of the monthly rent (or your share of the rent) on the budget worksheet.

   Apartments on Line
   http://www.rent.net/cgi-bin/rentnet

(continued)

Working for a Living *(continued)*

2. ***Transportation****.* For the purposes of this budget, let's assume that you will be buying a new car and financing (borrowing) the entire cost of the car. Go to the web site below. Pick out a car that you think will fit into your budget. Then go to the next web site and use that information to calculate your monthly payments. Once you know your payments, enter that amount on the budget worksheet. Use 8% for the annual percentage rate for the loan and four or five years for the period of the loan.

Pick out a car:
CarPoint
http://carpoint.msn.com   Car Selected: _____
or
Edmunds   Cost: _____
http://www.edmunds.com

Calculate monthly payment: Monthly payment: _____
Car Loan Calculator
http://www.edmunds.com/edweb/loan/calculator.html

3. ***Food****.* Since eating habits vary, it can be difficult to generalize about this expense. If you eat most of your meals at home and often bring your lunches from home, figure on spending about $50 a week on food. If you eat out a lot or eat a lot of prepared convenience foods, you might expect to spend closer to $100 a week on food. Another approach you might use is to ask your parents how much they spend on food. Enter what you think is an accurate amount on the budget worksheet.

4. ***Utilities****.* It's always nice when you flip on a light switch and the light actually comes on. Paying your utilities (electricity, water, gas) is a good idea, unless you don't mind reading in the dark or going without showers. Utility costs vary greatly, depending on where you live. Initially, budget 15% of your rent amount for utilities. Calculate that amount and enter it on the budget worksheet.

5. ***Phone****.* Basic phone service typically runs about $15 a month. However, the real cost of having a phone is making long distance calls. Long distance costs are directly proportional to how long you talk. Use this scale for figuring out your total phone costs. If you think you will make just a few long distance calls, add $10 to your bill; if you will make a few more, add $20 to your bill; if the phone is permanently attached to your ear, add $50. Enter the total amount on the budget worksheet.

6. ***Cable****.* Believe it or not, there was no cable television 30 years ago, and people just watched whatever was on the major networks. Times have changed, so if you think you can't live without cable, enter $35 on the budget worksheet.

(continued)

Working for a Living *(continued)*

7. ***Clothing.*** It's good to have clothes, but wouldn't you know it—they cost money. Often when you are fresh out of school or college and starting a new job, you have to buy a new wardrobe. Business clothes are very expensive. For now, set aside $75 a month for clothing.

8. ***Entertainment and Recreation.*** "All work and no play . . .," or so the saying goes, is not how you want to live. But don't forget to include these expenses in your budget. For now, enter $75 a month for entertainment and recreation expenses.

9. ***Student Loan Payment.*** Most people end up taking out a student loan while in college. Depending on where you go to school, loan amounts can be quite large. For your budget decide whether you will have graduated from a private or public college or university. Go to the web site below to calculate your loan payments, based on the following loans: $40,000–$80,000 for a private school and $10,000–$25,000 for a public institution. Enter the monthly payment on the budget worksheet. Use 7.5% for the annual percentage rate (APR), and select 10 years for the period of the loan.

    Student Loan Calculator
    http://www.studentloan.com/slcsite/fr_tools.htm

10. ***Savings.*** Savings isn't necessarily an expense, but it is something you have to allocate money for each month. Calculate the amount you put into savings each month at 5% of your monthly net income. Enter that amount on your budget worksheet.

11. ***Miscellaneous.*** When you make a budget, it's always a good idea to set aside some money for unforeseen and/or miscellaneous expenses, such as car repairs, gifts, etc. Set aside 2% of your monthly net income for miscellaneous expenses. Enter that amount on your budget worksheet.

Budget Analysis

1. What will your total expenses be for the entire year? _____

2. If your expenses are greater than your income, what expense would be easiest to lower to make your budget work? Explain.

    _____

    _____

    _____

    _____

(continued)

Working for a Living *(continued)*

3. Does your budget have room for you to increase your monthly savings amount to 8% of your income? Explain.

   _____

   _____

4. Suppose next month you get a raise of 3.1%. Which expense categories would you change, and by how much?

   _____

   _____

BUDGET WORKSHEET

Monthly Net Income	
Expenses	
Housing	
Transportation	
Food	
Utilities	
Phone	
Cable	
Clothing	
Entertainment and Recreation	
Student Loan	
Savings	
Miscellaneous	
Total Expenses	
Difference between Income and Expenses	

Road Trip

Overview:

In this lesson students will learn how to estimate the cost of a driving trip. Included in the budget will be gas, food, and lodging.

Learning Objectives:

- Use the Internet to obtain data for automobiles and calculate the average mpg.
- Calculate how much gas is needed and the cost of the gas.
- Estimate the price of meals.
- Calculate the total driving time, number of driving days, and number of nights; then find the total food and lodging costs.
- Calculate the total cost of each trip.

Web Sites:

Edmunds
http://www.edmunds.com

Microsoft CarPoint
http://carpoint.msn.com

Distance to Destinations
http://www.indo.com/distance

Free Trip (Prices for Hampton Inns)
http://www.freetrip.com

Choice Hotels (Comfort, Quality, EconoLodge, and Rodeway Inns)
http://www.hotelchoice.com/cgi-bin/res/webres?home.html

Materials:

Computer with Internet access; calculator

Suggestions:

1. This activity can be done by individual students, in pairs, or in small groups.

2. Gas prices fluctuate by region, so remind students that this is an estimation of actual costs.

3. Have students select new cars, since mpg figures for used cars are more difficult to obtain. Have students use highway mpg. You might also discuss how reliable these estimates are and why they may differ from actual mileage.

4. The destinations are suggestions. If you prefer, you or your students can select other destinations.

5. Some students have limited experience eating in restaurants. You may want to discuss meal costs with the class.

6. Review how to use the distance formula (d=rt) prior to using the lesson.

Selected Answers:

Answers will vary depending upon starting points and destinations.

Extensions:

Have students go to an airline web page to find out how much it would cost to fly to each destination. Then have them decide whether driving or flying would be more economical.

Road Trip

In this activity you will plan for a driving vacation to three of the most popular destinations in the United States. But before you hit the road, you have to know how much money to save for the trips. You need to estimate your traveling expenses—gas, food, lodging—to tell how much the trip will cost.

Fuel Costs

One of the first considerations when planning a trip is the cost of gas. To figure out how much you will spend on gas, you need to know three things: How much does gas cost per gallon? How many miles per gallon does your car get? How far do you have to go?

1. Find out how much a gallon of gas costs, and write the amount below.

   Price of one gallon of gas (unleaded): _____

2. Next, figure out how many miles per gallon (mpg) your car gets. For this activity you can pick any car you like. Go to one of the web sites below. Follow the pointers to find out how many miles per gallon the car gets.

   Edmunds   Microsoft CarPoint
   http://www.edmunds.com   http://carpoint.msn.com

   List the make, model, and mpg for your car: _____

3. Now find out how far each destination is from your hometown. To do this, go to the web site below. Enter your city as the starting point. Then enter each of the destinations in the table as the ending point. Remember, the distance given will be one-way only. You will have to double the distance to get round-trip miles. Next, make the calculations needed to fill in the rest of the table.

   Distance to Destinations
   http://www.indo.com/distance

GAS COSTS

Destination:	Distance in Miles (Round Trip)	Total Gallons of Gas Needed	Cost of Gas for the Trip
1. Grand Canyon			
2. Disney World (Orlando, FL.)			
3. Washington, D.C.			

(continued)

Road Trip *(continued)*

Food and Lodging

While you're on vacation you have to eat, and you may have to spend the night along the way. Follow the steps below to figure out your food and lodging expenses.

1. The price of food adds up quickly when you're on the road. Think about how much it cost the last time you ate a meal at a restaurant. Now consider that you might have to eat three meals a day in restaurants. Or, you might decide to pack a lunch or breakfast. Either way, you will have to plan for each meal in your vacation budget. List what you think your cost will be for each meal.

Breakfast: _____   Lunch: _____

Dinner: _____   Snacks: _____

Total cost of food per day: _____

2. To find out how many days and nights your trip will take, complete each section of the table below. Use the distance formula (d=rt) to determine how many hours each route will take. Assume that you will average 60 miles per hour and you will drive 9 hours per day.

DAYS OF DRIVING

Destination	Miles (Round Trip)	Mph	Total Hours	Hours Per Day	Number of Days	Number of Nights
1. Grand Canyon		60		9		
2. Disney World		60		9		
3. Washington, D.C.		60		9		

(continued)

Road Trip *(continued)*

3. The web pages below list prices for hotels. Visit each site and calculate the average hotel cost for the group. Use this amount for your lodging costs.

   Free Trip (Prices for Hampton Inns)   Price per night: _____
   http://www.freetrip.com

   Choice Hotels (Comfort, Quality, EconoLodge, and Rodeway Inns)
   http://www.hotelchoice.com/cgi-bin/res/webres?home.html

                                                 Price per night: _____

   Average Hotel Cost: _____

Total Cost

   Use the information from the two previous tables to complete the table below and determine the total cost of each trip.

Destination:	**Lodging**	**Food**	**Gas**	**Total Cost**
1. Grand Canyon				
2. Disney World				
3. Washington, D.C.				

1. Once you get to Washington, D.C., you decide to stay for five nights. How much will this add to the total cost of the vacation?

2. Would the cost of the trip to the Grand Canyon change if you drove for one more hour each day? Explain.

3. If you averaged 65 miles per hour on your way to Disney World, would your overall costs increase or decrease? Explain.

(continued)

Counting Heads

Overview:

In this lesson students will visit the U.S. Census Bureau "Pop Clock" over a 6-week period and use real-time data to make population projections.

Learning Objectives:

- Use the Internet to gather data and make population projections.
- Make computations based on data.
- Compare population projections with the actual figure from the U.S. Census Bureau.
- Calculate the weekly percentage of increase.
- Make long-range population projections.

Web Sites:

U.S. Census Bureau Pop Clock
http://www.census.gov/main/www/popclock.html

City Population
http://www.census.gov/cgi-bin/gazetteer

Materials:

Computer with Internet access; calculator; poster paper; stopwatch or timer

Suggestions:

1. This activity works well for both individual students and pairs of students. Before using this lesson, familiarize yourself with the table at the end of the lesson. Students may need guidance on where to enter their data.

2. Have students follow the steps below to complete the table:
   - Enter time and date in row one.
   - Go to U.S. Census Bureau web page, locate current census population amount, and enter figure in row one.
   - Convert that amount to scientific notation.
   - Wait 30 minutes (you may adjust time).
   - Record current census population amount in row two.
   - Convert to scientific notation.
   - Calculate percentage of population increase.
   - Use this information to estimate what population will be in one week.

   Next steps:
   - Enter time and date in table in row three.
   - Go to U.S. Census Bureau web page, locate current census population amount, and enter in row three.
   - Convert that amount to scientific notation.
   - Calculate percentage of population increase.
   - Use this information to estimate what population will be in one week.

3. For rows four through seven, repeat the steps for row three; be sure to enter data on the correct lines of the table.

4. Percentage of increase should be calculated using the U.S. Census Bureau's population amounts, not the student's estimates.

5. When students are making population estimates, they may choose either to set up and solve proportions or to multiply using the percentage of increase.

Selected Answers:

Answers will vary depending on population amounts and time intervals.

Extensions:

This lesson can be modified to be used with world population data, which is available through the Census Bureau's web site.

Counting Heads

Every 10 years the U.S. Census Bureau determines the population of the United States. Suppose you had the job of helping them. Where would you start? Would you have to count every single person in the United States, or is that even possible? It is probably impossible. So what can you do? If you said "estimate," you are right. Work through the steps below to help the Census Bureau with your population estimation.

United States Population Predictions

A. Week 1

1. The U.S. Census Bureau has a web page where it continually updates an estimate of the U.S. population. This population estimate is based on the 1990 census. Go to the web page below. Select Current U.S. Population Count. Record the date, time, and current population amount for the United States in row 1 of the table on the last page of this handout. Then convert the current population to scientific notation. You will be using this table over the next few weeks, so be sure to hold on to it.

   U.S. Census Bureau Pop Clock
   http://www.census.gov/main/www/popclock.html

2. Wait exactly 30 minutes. Go back to the U.S. Census Bureau Pop Clock page. Record the current population amount in row 2 of the table. Then convert the current population to scientific notation. Also, determine the percentage of population increase during that period of time.

3. Based on the population difference and the percentage of population increase over the last 30 minutes, estimate what the population will be in one week (7 days) from the first time you recorded the population (row 1 of the table). Record your estimate in the Your Population Projection column of row 3 of the table.

B. Week 2

1. Exactly one week later (to the minute if possible) from your first visit to the Pop Clock, go back to the Pop Clock page. Record the population amount in row 3 of your table. Convert to scientific notation. Compare your prediction with the U.S. Census Bureau's information. How close was your prediction to theirs? Explain.

_____

_____

_____

(continued)

Counting Heads *(continued)*

2. Calculate the percentage of increase for that period. Record the result in row 3 under percentage of population increase in your table.

C. Weeks 3–6

1. Once again, make a projection of what the population will be in exactly one week. Write your projection in row 4 of your table. In exactly one-week intervals, visit the Pop Clock web site, record the population in the table, and make a projection about the population for the next week. How accurate are your projections? Are you getting more accurate? Explain.

_____

_____

_____

After You Have Completed Your Six-Week Study

1. Visit the web site below to find out the population of the city you live in. Using that information, and what you have learned from observing the United States population over the last six weeks, estimate the population of your city in 1 year, 5 years, and 20 years.

City Population
http://www.census.gov/cgi-bin/gazetteer

Current Population (based on 1990 census): _____

Population in 1 year: _____

Population in 5 years: _____

Population in 20 years: _____

2. Describe some of the factors that might account for population growth or population decline in your city. Are these factors the same for all cities? Explain.

_____

_____

_____

(continued)

Counting Heads *(continued)*

3. What are two different methods you can use to make accurate projections of the population?

_____

_____

Displaying Your Results

Organize the data from your population projections for your city on poster paper by creating a chart, graph, or table. Try to make the data visually interesting, and remember to label your table and graphs and to use appropriate legends. You may want to use a computer graphing program to help you.

	Date/Time	Your Population Projection	U.S. Census Bureau Population Figure	U.S. Census Bureau Prediction (SCI Notation)	Percentage of Increase
1		N/A			N/A
2 (30 minutes later)		N/A			
3 (one week after line 1)					
4 (one week after line 3)					
5 (one week after line 4)					
6 (one week after line 5)					
7 (one week after line 6)					

Games, Games, and More Games

Overview:

In this lesson students investigate interactive game sites, such as Tic-Tac-Toe and Connect Four. As they play the games, students keep track of wins and losses and answer questions based on those results.

Learning Objectives:

- Play games and keep track of wins, losses, and the times of the games.
- Collect and analyze data.
- Solve problems based on their win/loss records.

Web Sites:

Tic-Tac-Toe
http://www.boulter.com/ttt

Connect!
http://www.cs.monash.edu.au/cgi-bin/cgiwrap/dcron/connect_www.cgi

Scrambler
http://www.edbydesign.com/scramble.html

Materials:

Computer with Internet access; calculator; stopwatch or timer

Suggestions:

1. Students may work individually or in pairs, alternating playing the games and acting as timekeeper.

2. Little explanation to students is necessary for most to begin playing the games. If more information is needed, either you can explain the rules or direct students to the web sites themselves for explanation.

3. As an introduction to this activity, ascertain from students what connections they might see between playing games and math.

4. When students are playing Tic-Tac-Toe, encourage them to select more difficult settings, such as four or five in a row to win.

Selected Answers:

Answers will vary depending on win/loss records and the time it takes to solve the puzzles.

Extensions:

There are many game web sites on the Internet; most deal with commercial videogame types, but with a little persistence, you will locate more games that are appropriate for the classroom.

Games, Games, and More Games

Can you imagine your teacher asking you, "Since you all have worked so hard in class, why don't we take a break and play some games?" Before you say, "No way, that will never happen," take a look at this activity.

Tic-Tac-Toe

The web site below is an interactive Tic-Tac-Toe game. It allows you to set parameters, such as the size of the board and how many in a row you need to win. Go to the web site. Practice playing some games and changing the settings.

Tic-Tac-Toe
http://www.boulter.com/ttt

Now that you are comfortable playing the game, decide on the settings (at least four in a row to win) and play 10 games. Keep track of your wins and losses. Then answer the questions that follow.

Game	1	2	3	4	5	6	7	8	9	10	Total
Won											
Lost											

1. Calculate your percentage of winning games: _____

2. If you played 10 more games, predict what your overall win/loss record would be.

   _____

3. If you played 100 games, would your winning percentage change? Explain.

   _____

   _____

Connect Four

Go to the Connect Four web site below and practice playing some games.

Connect!
http://www.cs.monash.edu.au/cgi-bin/cgiwrap/dcron/connect_www.cgi

Once you are comfortable with playing the game, play 10 games. Keep track of wins and losses. Then answer the questions that follow.

(continued)

Name _____ Date _____

Games, Games, and More Games *(continued)*

Game	1	2	3	4	5	6	7	8	9	10	Total
Won											
Lost											

1. Calculate your winning percentage: _____

2. How many more wins or losses would you need in order to have a winning percentage

   of 60%? _____ What about a winning percentage of 85%?

   _____

Scrambler

When you are playing Scrambler, you don't necessarily win or lose; you either solve the puzzle or you don't. Go to the Scrambler web site. Keep track of how long it takes you to solve five puzzles. Then answer the questions that follow.

Scrambler
http://www.edbydesign.com/scramble.html

Puzzles Solved:	1	2	3	4	5
Times:					

1. What was the average time it took you to solve a puzzle? _____

2. Assuming you did nothing but sit in front of the computer 24 hours a day and solve

   puzzles, how many would you be able to solve in a day? _____

   A week? _____ A year? _____

More Game Sites

Listed below are some game sites that you might be interested in checking out.

Yahtzee
http://www.yahoo.com/Recreation/Games/Board_Games/Yahtzee/Web_Based/
Othello
http://www.atmedia.net/TWWEP/othello.cgi/guest/small/?newgame

Paint the Classroom

Teacher Guide

Overview:

In this activity students will assume the role of a general contractor. As contractors, they will actively work through a process to generate a bid to paint a classroom.

Learning Objectives:

- Organize and gather information in a systematic process to arrive at a finished product.

- Apply geometric principles to work-related situations.

- Use estimation as a tool to determine costs.

- Evaluate available information and use that information as a basis to make informed decisions.

Web Sites:

Home Depot Store Locator
http://www.homedepot.com

Sears
http://www.sears.com/

Homearts Paint Estimator
http://homearts.com/cgi-bin/estimate/submit.pl?Rectangular+Paint

Better Homes and Gardens Paint Estimator
http://www.bhg.com/homeimp/calculators/paint.html

Livinghome Paint Estimator
http://www.livinghome.net/cgi-bin/nph-ep?J61S61D57265

Conversion Factor Table
http://www.wctc.net/~wallin/convert

Materials:

Computer with Internet access; tape measure, ruler, or meter stick; calculator

Suggestions:

1. This activity should be done in pairs or small groups.

2. If this lesson is used with "Carpet the Classroom," have students combine the bid amounts and make one overall bid.

3. A gallon of paint should cost about $15.

4. Home Depot and Sears are just two possible sources of prices. You can look at newspapers or use other stores in the area.

5. Familiarize yourself with how to use the different paint estimators so that you can answer student questions as they arise.

6. It is crucial that students justify their bid amount.

Selected Answers:

Answers will vary depending on classroom size and the cost of paint.

Extensions:

Collect and post students' bid amounts, and have the class decide which bid would most likely be selected.

Name _____   Date _____

Paint the Classroom

Suppose you and your partner(s) are general contractors who want to bid on a remodeling job for your school. The job involves repainting 10 classrooms (all the same size) at your school. In order to get the job, your group must submit a bid lower than any of the other contractors' bids, but it must be high enough to ensure that you will make a profit. You will use the Internet to find out costs for paint and to verify your estimation of needed materials. Follow the steps below to arrive at your final bid.

Determine Your Fixed Costs

1. Find out how much a gallon of paint costs by visiting the web sites below and finding the store nearest you. Once you have located the nearest store, visit or call them for prices. Ask the sales person for a range of prices based on quality of the paint. Explain that the paint should be appropriate for a classroom setting. Other costs, such as labor and painting supplies, are given.

Home Depot Store Locator
http://www.HomeDepot.com
(click on store locator)

Sears
http://www.sears.com/storeloc/floc.htm
(click on store locator)

Paint:
Average cost of paint (per gallon): _____

Painting supplies (per room): <u>$25</u>   Labor: <u>$50 per room</u>

Painting Costs

Start by measuring the surface area of the walls. Be sure to take into account the spaces that won't be painted, such as windows, bulletin boards, bookshelves, cabinets, and writing surfaces.

1. Organize the measurements for the walls using the table on the next page.

2. Calculate the number of gallons of paint you will need for each room. One gallon of paint should cover approximately 300 sq. ft. Show your work in the space provided.

Number of gallons per room: _____

(continued)

         Using the Internet to Investigate Math

Paint the Classroom *(continued)*

	Base (ft.)	Height (ft.)	Surface Area of the Wall (sq. ft.)	Amount of Space Not to Be Painted (sq. ft.)	Total Area of the Wall to Be Painted (sq. ft.)
Front Wall					
Back Wall					
Side Wall					
Side Wall					

Total Surface Area to Be Painted (sq. ft.)

3. The three web sites listed below are on-line paint estimators. Each paint estimator will calculate the number of gallons of paint you need for a painting job. Go to each paint estimator, supply the requested information, and have the estimator calculate the required number of gallons of paint. As the results are given, fill in the table.

Homearts Paint Estimator
http://homearts.com/cgi-bin/estimate/submit.pl?Rectangular+Paint

Better Homes and Gardens Paint Estimator
http://www.bhg.com/homeimp/calculators/paint.html

Livinghome Paint Estimator
http://www.livinghome.net/cgi-bin/nph-ep?J61S61D57265

PAINT ESTIMATORS

	Paint Estimator One (Homearts)	Paint Estimator Two (Better Homes and Gardens)	Paint Estimator Three (Livinghome)	Your Estimate
Gallons of Paint Needed per Room				

(continued)

Paint the Classroom *(continued)*

4. You now have four different recommendations for the amount of paint you need. How would you decide how much paint to buy? Explain.

    _____

    _____

5. Calculate the cost of paint for each room using the pricing information and the number of gallons of paint needed.

    Cost of paint per room: _____

6. Figure out the total cost of painting a room using the cost of paint, labor, and supplies.

    Total cost of painting a room: _____

7. Write and solve an equation that shows the total cost of painting all 10 rooms.

Total Cost for Painting 10 Rooms

1. Look back over your work. Figure out how much it will cost to paint one room and all 10 rooms.

    Total cost to paint one room: _____

    Total cost to paint all 10 rooms: _____

2. Often there are unforeseen costs. Add 10% to your total cost to account for this.

    Total cost plus 10%: _____

3. Based on the total cost (plus 10%), determine what you will bid. Remember, you will need to be competitive by keeping costs to a minimum, but you also have to make a profit. Show your reasoning. Explain how you determined your bid amount.

Carpet the Classroom

Overview:

In this activity students will assume the role of a general contractor. As contractors, they will actively work through a process to generate a bid to carpet a classroom.

Learning Objectives:

- Organize and gather information in a systematic process to arrive at a finished product.
- Apply geometric principles to work-related situations.
- Use estimation as a tool to determine costs.
- Evaluate available information and use that information as a basis to make informed decisions.

Web Sites:

Home Depot Store Locator
http://www.homedepot.com

Sears
http://www.sears.com/

Conversion Factor Table
http://www.wctc.net/~wallin/convert

Materials:

Computer with Internet access; tape measure, ruler, or meter stick; grid paper; calculator

Suggestions:

1. This activity should be done in pairs or small groups.
2. If this lesson is used with "Paint the Classroom," have students combine the bid amounts and make one overall bid.
3. Carpet should be about $10 a square yard.
4. If the classroom doesn't have carpet, have students figure the cost of carpet removal anyway.
5. Home Depot and Sears are just two possible sources of prices. You can look at newspapers or use other stores in the area.
6. It is crucial that students justify their bid amount.

Selected Answers:

Answers will vary depending on classroom size and the cost of carpet.

Extensions:

Collect and post students' bid amounts, and have the class decide which bid would most likely be selected.

Name _____   Date _____

Carpet the Classroom

Suppose you and your partner(s) are general contractors who want to bid on a remodeling job. The job involves recarpeting ten classrooms (all the same size) at your school. In order to get the job, your group must submit a bid lower than any of the other contractors' bids, but it must be high enough to ensure that you will make a profit. Use the Internet to find out costs for carpet and to verify your estimation of materials. Follow the steps below to arrive at your final bid.

Determine Your Fixed Costs

1. Find out how much a square yard of carpet costs by visiting the web sites below to find the store nearest you. Once you have located the nearest store, visit or call them for prices. Ask the sales person for a range of prices based on the grade of the carpet. Explain that the carpet should be appropriate for a classroom setting. Other costs, such as labor, are given.

   Home Depot Store Locator   Sears
   http://www.HomeDepot.com   http://www.sears.com

   Carpet:

   Average cost of carpet (per square yd.) _____

   Labor: $4.00 per sq. yd.   Remove old carpet: $0.35 per sq. yd.

Carpet Costs

1. Measure the length and width of your classroom floor and record the results below.

   Length: _____   Width: _____

2. In order to figure out how much carpet you need per room, do you need to find the area or do you need to find the perimeter of the room? Explain which you selected. Then do the necessary calculations and record the figure here. _____

3. Many classrooms are irregularly shaped. To help you organize your information, make a scale drawing of the floor of your classroom on a piece of grid paper.

(continued)

Carpet the Classroom *(continued)*

4. The cost of carpet is given in square yards, so you must convert the unit of measure that you used to yards. Go to the web page below to find the conversion factor for changing the unit of measurement you used into yards. Then make the necessary conversions.

   Conversion Factor Table
   http://www.wctc.net/~wallin/convert   Conversion factor (cf.): _____

   Total number of square yards needed for one classroom: _____

5. If you measured the length and width of your classroom and then calculated the area using feet, explain how you would convert that amount to square yards.

   _____

   _____

6. The cost of one square yard of carpet equals the price of the carpet (padding included) plus the price of labor. Calculate the cost of each square yard of carpet: _____

7. The cost to remove the old carpet is $0.35 per square yard. Calculate the cost to remove the existing carpet: _____

8. Write an equation that shows the total cost to install the new carpet and remove the old carpet. Then write an equation that shows the total cost for one classroom.

   Total cost of carpet per square yard: _____

   Total cost of carpet per classroom: _____

Total Cost for Carpeting Ten Rooms

1. Look back over your work and figure out how much it will cost to carpet one room and all 10 rooms. List your answers below.

   Total cost to carpet one room: _____

   Total cost to carpet all 10 rooms: _____

2. Often there are unforeseen costs. Add 10% to your total cost to account for these.

   Total cost plus 10%: _____

3. Based on the total cost (plus 10%), determine what you are going to bid. Remember, you will need to be competitive by keeping costs to a minimum, but you also have to make a profit. Show your reasoning and explain how you determined your bid amount.

Measuring Your Fitness Level

Overview:

In this activity students will calculate their body fat percentages and body mass indexes and use that information to gauge their fitness levels.

Learning Objectives:

- Take accurate measurements and use that information to make calculations.
- Collect and analyze data.
- Make judgments about fitness levels.

Web Sites:

Body Fat Calculator for Men
http://www.top.monad.net/~vsi/java/mbf/mbf_calc.html

Body Fat Calculator for Women
http://www.top.monad.net/~vsi/java/wbf/bf_calc.html

Shape Up America Body Mass Index
http://www.shapeup.org/bmi/index.html

Interactive Conversion Table
http://www.mplik.ru/~sg/transl/index.html

Are You Overweight
http://www.arachnoid.com/ (search for "Are you overweight?")

Materials:

Computer with Internet access; tape measure; calculator; scale; index cards

Suggestions:

1. This activity should be done in same-sex pairs or small groups.

2. This activity can be done in coordination with a unit on health or with the help of the physical education teachers.

3. To avoid embarrassment for some students, you may choose to throw out the highest and lowest body fat percentages.

4. Stress the importance of taking accurate measurements.

5. Use the scale in the gym to obtain students' weights.

Selected Answers:

Answers will vary depending on students' measurements.

Extensions:

Coordinate with the physical education department and have students measure their times to run one mile. Use that information to find each student's VO_{2max}, which is a measure of how much oxygen your body uses during aerobic exercise. Go to the web page below and follow the directions for finding your VO_{2max}.

VO_{2max} Calculator
http://www.runnersweb.com/running/VO2.shtml

Measuring Your Fitness Level

In this activity you will use two different tools to gauge your level of fitness—body fat percentage and body mass index (BMI).

Body Fat Percentage

One way athletes measure their fitness levels is by finding their body fat percentages. Some athletes, such as male bodybuilders, have body fat percentages as low as 3 or 4 percent. More commonly, a male athlete might have a body fat percentage around 12–13 percent. Female athletes, and females in general, tend to have slightly higher body fat percentages. Typically, a male in good physical condition should have a body fat percentage under 22 percent, while a female should have less than 25 percent. Find out what your body fat percentage is by completing the steps below.

1. With your partner or in your group, for males, measure your wrist and waist (at the navel); for females, measure your waist (at the navel) and hips (9 inches below waist). Take each measurement (to the nearest quarter-inch) three times. Average them to improve accuracy. Record your results below.

   Waist (both males and females)

   1. _____ 2. _____ 3. _____ Waist average: _____

   Wrist (males only)

   1. _____ 2. _____ 3. _____ Wrist average: _____

   Hips (females only)

   1. _____ 2. _____ 3. _____ Hips average: _____

2. Go to the appropriate web site below and enter your measurements into the body fat calculator. Record your results.

   Body Fat Calculator for Men
   http://www.top.monad.net/~vsi/java/mbf/mbf_calc.html

   Body Fat Calculator for Women
   http://www.top.monad.net/~vsi/java/wbf/bf_calc.html

   Your body fat percentage: _____ male—female (circle one)

3. Write your results on an index card and turn it in to your teacher.

(continued)

Name _____   Date _____

Measuring Your Fitness Level *(continued)*

4. Once the teacher has collected and posted all the body fat percentages for the class, use that information to calculate the mean, median, mode, and range for the male students, female students, and the entire class.

BODY FAT PERCENTAGES

	Mean	**Median**	**Mode**	**Range**
Male Students				
Female Students				
All Students				

5. On the back of this page, construct a bar graph that shows the comparison of body fat percentages for each group.

Body Mass Index

Body mass index is not as widely used as body fat percentage; however, it is still a good indicator of your fitness level. Follow these steps to determine your BMI.

1. Learn more about why your BMI is an important indicator of your fitness level by visiting the web site below. (Click on the section marked "Why is BMI important?")

   Shape Up America—Body Mass Index
   http://www.shapeup.org/bmi/index.html

2. In order to find your BMI, you first have to measure your height and weight. With your partner or in your group, measure each other's height in inches and record the results below. Likewise, weigh yourself in pounds and record the results below.

   Height (inches): _____   Weight (pounds): _____

3. The formula used to calculate your BMI requires metric units. To convert your height and weight into metric units, go to the conversion web site below.

   Interactive Conversion Table
   http://www.mplik.ru/~sg/transl/index.html

   Height (meters): _____   Weight (kilograms): _____

(continued)

                                       Using the Internet to Investigate Math

Measuring Your Fitness Level *(continued)*

4. Calculate your BMI using the formula below.

$$BMI = \frac{Weight\ (kg)}{Height\ (m)^2}$$

BMI = _____

5. Use one of the web pages below to verify the accuracy of your BMI calculation.

Are You Overweight
http://www.arachnoid.com/ (search for: "Are you overweight?")

or

Shape Up America—Body Mass Index
http://www.shapeup.org/bmi/index.html (Click on Start BMI.)

6. Turn your BMI results in to your teacher on an index card.

7. Once the teacher has collected and posted all the body mass indexes for the class, use that information to calculate the mean, median, mode, and range for the male students, female students, and the entire class.

BODY MASS INDEX

	Mean	**Median**	**Mode**	**Range**
Male Students				
Female Students				
All Students				

7. According to the body fat percentages and the BMI's of the students in your class, how would you rate the fitness level of your class? Explain.

_____

_____

_____

What to Do with All Our Garbage?

Overview:

In this activity students will use the Internet to learn more about recycling. They will devise a plan to collect, measure, and sort the recycling products they collect in their classroom. Then they will use the Internet to gather important facts and solve problems about recycling paper, aluminum, and glass.

Learning Objectives:

- Perform calculations to determine the impact of a recycling program for the class.
- Design a flyer advertising their recycling program.

Web Sites:

Commonly Recycled Materials
http://www.obviously.com/recycle

Paper Factoids
http://ecosys.drdr.virginia.edu/
paperfac.html

Aluminum Factoids
http://ecosys.drdr.virginia.edu/
alumfac.html

Glass Factoids
http://ecosys.drdr.virginia.edu/
glassfac.html

Materials

Computer with Internet access; protractor; compass; disposable gloves; tape measure, yard-sticks, or meter sticks; plastic bags or cardboard boxes to sort recycled material; scale

Suggestions:

1. This activity works best for students working in small groups.

2. If your school already has a recycling program in place, have your students use this lesson in conjunction with the current program. If there is no recycling program, you will need to help students set up their classroom recycling program.

3. Many web sites deal with recycling. The sites used for this lesson are general. If you need more detailed information, conduct further searches.

4. When students are collecting recycling material, have them sort it daily.

5. When students are answering questions about specific recycling materials, have them make their calculations based on the amount of material collected in the classroom.

6. Have each group measure and weigh the recycled material at the end of the week.

Selected Answers:

Learn more about recycling:

1. 1 and 2, sometimes 4
2. 1-800 Motor Oil
3. Clear glass
4. Mixed paper, paper contaminated with food, waxed paper, carbon, tissues, juice boxes, pet food bags, and laminated paper
5. Poisons, paints, oil, solvents, auto fluids, cleaners, and herbicides. Other answers will vary depending on how much recycling material is gathered.

Extensions:

Have students write a letter asking the principal to support a recycling program.

What to Do with All Our Garbage?

Suppose that you and some of your friends at school are concerned about the amount of trash the school generates. You wonder if there is anything you can do. The group decides that, like a lot of schools, businesses, and homes, you should have a recycling program. But how do you know that a recycling program really works? Will the principal, teachers, and other students think that the school needs a recycling program? These are a lot of questions to answer. So you and your friends decide to become recycling experts to convince the other people at your school that a recycling program would save valuable resources.

Learn More about Recycling

The first step in planning your recycling program is to learn more about the basics of recycling. Go to the web site below and answer the following questions.

Commonly Recycled Materials
http://www.obviously.com/recycle

1. Plastic marked with what numbers is best for recycling?

   _____

2. What is the phone number for locating the nearest disposal location for used motor oil?

   _____

3. Which type of glass is the most valuable for recycling?

   _____

4. Name some different types of paper that *cannot* be recycled.

   _____

5. Name some items that should *not* be dumped into regular household garbage.

   _____

From Classrooms to Landfills, What Do Your School's Recycled Materials Look Like?

Now that you are an expert on the subject of recycling, you and your friends decide that you need to know more about what your school is actually throwing away. Set up a recycling program in your classroom to collect paper, aluminum cans, and glass containers. Sort the

(continued)

What to Do with All Our Garbage? *(continued)*

material that is collected daily, and at the end of the week, weigh the paper, aluminum cans, and glass. You will also need to measure the volume of the glass and count the number of aluminum cans.

RECYCLED MATERIAL COLLECTED FOR THE WEEK

Paper (Weight in Pounds)	Glass (Volume and Weight)	Aluminum Cans (Number of Cans and Weight)

Go to the web pages below. Use the information from your table to answer the questions that follow.

Paper

Paper Factoids
http://ecosys.drdr.virginia.edu/paperfac.html

1. For your class, how many trees will be used for paper during the school year? What about for the whole school? _____

2. How many cubic feet of landfill would be saved by recycling paper at your school?

   _____

3 Assuming the school is not recycling its paper, how many gallons of oil will be used to make the paper your class uses in a year? _____

Aluminum

Aluminum Factoids
http://ecosys.drdr.virginia.edu/alumfac.html

1. In one year, how many aluminum cans would you expect to be recycled by your class?

   _____

2. If you placed the aluminum cans on their sides end to end, how many feet would the cans stretch in one year? _____

(continued)

What to Do with All Our Garbage? *(continued)*

3. In one year, how many barrels of oil would your class save through its aluminum recycling program? _____

Glass

Glass Factoids
http://ecosys.drdr.virginia.edu/glassfac.html

1. How long would it take to fill up your classroom with glass containers that are recycled by your class? _____

2. How many pounds of feldspar would be conserved if your class recycled its glass containers? _____

Advertise Your Program

On a separate piece of paper, design a flyer or brochure to encourage other students and teachers to participate in your recycling program. Include as many facts and as much information as you need to gain support for a recycling program at your school.

Counting Calories

Overview:

In this activity students will keep track of the foods they eat for one day and then use the Internet to determine how many calories and fat grams they eat per day.

Learning Objectives:

- Use the Internet to define terms and learn more about the information contained on food labels.

- Use a table to keep track of the foods eaten in one day.

- Calculate the average number of calories and grams of fat eaten in a day.

- Collect data for the class and find the average number of calories eaten and grams of fat used in a day.

- Organize the foods eaten and display them using a circle graph.

- Display the data.

Web Sites:

Reading Food Labels
http://www.fda.gov/fdac/special/foodlabel/facts.html

Reading Food Labels
http://www.caloriecontrol.org/

Calories in Various Foods
http://www.fourmilab.ch/hackdiet/www/chapter1_4_3.html

Nutritional Values for Foods
http://www.mcs.anl.gov/otc/Guide/CaseStudies/diet/complete_table.html

Categories of Foods
http://www.ganesa.com/food/index.html

Materials:

Computer with Internet access; calculator; poster paper

Suggestions:

1. Students can work individually or in pairs for this lesson.

2. Have students collect labels from the foods they eat for several days prior to starting this activity.

3. For background information about health and nutrition topics, search: http://www.yahoo.com/Health/.

4. Students will need further guidance on how to estimate calories for prepared foods, especially on how to determine portion size.

Selected Answers:

Answers will vary depending on what foods are eaten.

Extensions:

Have students keep track of the foods they eat over an extended period of time, such as a week.

Counting Calories

Have you ever known someone who was counting calories? Chances are you have. People count calories for many reasons—some want to lose weight, others want to gain weight, and some people just like to keep track of what they are eating. But what does it mean to "count calories," and how do they affect us? Follow the steps below to find the answers to some of these questions.

Food Labels

Begin by taking a closer look at what you eat. As you look at the labels on the foods you eat during the day, you will notice that they contain a lot of information and numbers. To help you understand what those labels mean, go to one of the web sites below. Find the answers to the following four questions.

Reading Food Labels
http://vm.cfsan.fda.gov/label.html   or   http://www.caloriecontrol.org/

1. How many calories are in one gram of fat? _____

2. List the items that are mandatory components on a food label:

   _____

   _____

3. How many calories are the daily percentages based on? _____

4. How many calories are there in one pound of fat?_____

Vocabulary

Now that you have a better understanding of how to read food labels, learn more about some of the terms that are used on them. Using the same web sites as above, find the definitions for the following words:

Calorie: _____

Carbohydrate: _____

Cholesterol: _____

Protein: _____

(continued)

Counting Calories *(continued)*

How Many Calories Do You Eat in a Day?

To figure out how many calories and fat grams you eat in a day, use the table below to keep track of what you eat, and the calories and fat in each food. At the end of the day find the total number of calories and fat grams you ate. Some of the foods you eat will be prepared (for instance, meals you eat in the cafeteria), so you will have to estimate how many calories and fat grams they contain. Use the tables on the web sites below and the labels on the foods to find out how many calories and fat grams are in the foods you ate.

Nutritional Values for Foods
http://www.mcs.anl.gov/otc/Guide/CaseStudies/diet/complete_table.html

Calories in Various Foods
http://www.fourmilab.ch/hackdiet/www/chapter1_4_3.html

CALORIES AND FAT GRAMS

Breakfast Foods	Calories	Fat Grams	Dinner Foods	Calories	Fat Grams
Lunch Foods	**Calories**	**Fat Grams**	**Snacks**	**Calories**	**Fat Grams**

Total calories for the day: _____   Total grams of fat for the day: _____

Class Data

Collect data for the calories per day and the number of grams of fat per day for the entire class. Then calculate the class average for each of those categories. List the calories eaten per day and the grams of fat eaten per day for each student on the data table on the next page.

(continued)

Counting Calories *(continued)*

CLASS DATA

Calories eaten per day	
Grams of fat per day	

1. What is the class average for number of calories eaten per day? _____

2. What is the class average for number of fat grams eaten per day? _____

3. How do the class averages compare to your daily amounts? Explain.

_____

_____

What Kinds of Foods Are You Eating?

Carefully examine the types of food you ate during the day. Organize them by category; you can find help in doing this by visiting the web site below. When you are finished categorizing your foods, create a circle graph on a piece of poster paper that displays the percent you ate of each food category.

Categories of Foods
http://www.ganesa.com/food/index.html

Calorie Questions

1. Suppose you wanted to lose 10 pounds over the next 20 weeks in even intervals. How many fewer calories per day would you have to eat in order to lose the 10 pounds?

_____

2. How many calories do you eat in a week? _____

A year? _____   A lifetime? _____

Burning Calories

Overview:

In this lesson students keep track of their physical activities over the course of a day and compare that information with the foods they eat.

Learning Objectives:

- Use a table to keep track of physical activities for one day.
- Use the Internet to find out how many calories each activity burns.
- Calculate the total number of calories they use in a day.
- Collect data for the class and find the average number of calories burned in a day.
- Organize the activities and display them using a circle graph.
- Display the data.

Web Sites:

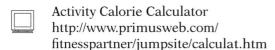

Activity Calorie Calculator
http://www.primusweb.com/
fitnesspartner/jumpsite/calculat.htm

Materials:

Computer with Internet access; calculator; poster paper

Suggestions:

1. Students should keep track of their own physical activities but can work together on collecting and analyzing the class data.

2. This lesson should be done after students have completed the "Counting Calories" lesson.

3. Some students may need help setting up proportions for determining calorie expenditures.

4. Review with students how to convert minutes to hours.

Selected Answers:

Answers will vary depending on the students' physical activities for the day.

Extensions:

Have students keep track of their physical activities over an extended period of time, such as a week.

Burning Calories

If you want to gain or lose weight, keeping track of the calories you eat is only half of the story. You also need to know how many calories you burn each day. Use the table labeled "Calories Used per Day" to keep track of your activities for one day. To figure out how many calories each activity uses, go to the web page below.

Activity Calorie Calculator
http://www.primusweb.com/fitnesspartner/jumpsite/calculat.htm

1. Total number of calories needed per day: _____

2. Actual number of calories you burn in one day: _____

CALORIES USED PER DAY

Activity	Total Time Spent Doing Activity (in Hours)	×	Calories Used per Hour for Your Body Weight	=	Calories Used for That Activity

Total calories burned in day:

(continued)

Burning Calories *(continued)*

3. Compare the number of calories you eat on a typical day with the number of calories you burn on a typical day. Based on the number of calories you eat and the number of calories you burn in a day, would you expect to gain weight, lose weight, or stay the same if you continue to eat as you do now? Explain.

_____

_____

Class Data

Collect the number of calories used per day for each student in the class. For each student, list the calories used per day on the data table below. Once you have collected the data for the entire class, calculate the class average.

CLASS DATA

Calories used per day	

1. What is the class average for number of calories burned per day? _____

2. How does the class average compare to your level? Explain. _____

_____

_____

Physical Activities

Carefully examine your physical activities for the day and organize them into categories. On a piece of poster paper, create a circle graph that displays the percent of time spent on each activity.

Summary

You have collected a significant amount of data during this activity. Figure out the best way to display your data. You may want to draw pictures, make tables, graphs, or charts, or draw scatter plots. You might also want to use a computer to create a spreadsheet. However you decide to display your data, conclude your presentation by summarizing your findings.

Cooking in Metric

Teacher Guide

Overview:

In this activity students use the Internet to find recipes and then convert them to metric measures.

Learning Objectives:

- Utilize correct conversion factors.
- Convert from customary to metric units.
- Set up and solve proportions.

Web Sites:

Cyber Kitchen
http://www.cyber-kitchen.com

Hershey's
http://www.hersheys.com/cookbook

Conversion Factor Table
http://www.wctc.net/~wallin/convert/cvert.html

Jell-O Jigglers
http://www.kraftfood.com/jell-o/world/recipeframe.html

Materials:

Computer with Internet access; calculator; hot plate; water (about 10 cups); gelatin dessert (about eight 8-ounce packages); measuring cup (must have metric units); optional: decorative cookie cutters

Suggestions:

1. This activity can be done individually, in pairs, or in small groups.

2. Have students change fractions to decimals before converting recipe amounts.

3. Students may be confused about how to use conversion factors, so you may want to work through several examples during the lesson.

4. Making the Jell-O Jigglers™ can be messy; if possible, use a room that is well equipped to handle a mess.

5. Jigglers™ need to set for at least 3 hours.

5. The Jigglers™ recipe can be used with almost any mold or cookie cutters to make any shape you like.

Selected Answers:

Conversion factors:

1. 14.79
2. 4.93
3. 0.9463
4. 0.4731765
5. 0.02957
6. 0.4536
7. 28.35

Extensions:

There are a number of recipe conversion calculators that will make adjustments for serving size.

Recipe Conversion Calculator
http://www.monomoy.com/metric.htm

Cooking in Metric

Recipes often list ingredients using fractions. Wouldn't it be easier if recipes were given using the metric system so that you wouldn't have to deal with fractions? Or would it? Work through the investigation below and decide for yourself which would be easier, fractions or the metric system.

Pick Your Recipes

What's your favorite dish? Is it a dessert, like brownies or cookies, or a meat dish, such as meatloaf? Whatever your favorite food is, you can find a recipe for it on the Internet. Go to one of the web sites below and choose three recipes. Enter the ingredients, number of servings, and amounts in your table labeled "Recipes."

Cyber Kitchen
http://www.cyber-kitchen.com

or

Hershey's
http://www.hersheys.com/cookbook

Conversion Factor

A conversion factor is not how many times a football team converts on third down. It is a number that you multiply one unit of measure by to convert it into another unit of measure. For instance, if you were converting from tablespoons to milliliters in a recipe that calls for two tablespoons, you would need to multiply the number of tablespoons (2) by the conversion factor (c.f.) in order to get milliliters.

Go to the conversion factor web site below. Look up the conversion factors to convert from customary to metric units. List the conversion factors in the "Conversion Factor Table." Then make the conversions for your recipes. Enter the amounts in the appropriate section of the "Recipe" table.

Conversion Factor Table
http://www.wctc.net/~wallin/convert/cvert.html

(continued)

Cooking in Metric *(continued)*

RECIPES

Recipe One:

Ingredients and Number of Servings:	Amount	Metric Measure

Recipe Two:

Ingredients and Number of Servings:	Amount	Metric Measure

Recipe Three:

Ingredients and Number of Servings:	Amount	Metric Measure

CONVERSION FACTOR TABLE

To Convert from:	to:	Conversion Factor (c.f.):
Tablespoons	Milliliters	
Teaspoons	Milliliters	
Quarts (liquid)	Liters	
Pints (liquid)	Liters	
Ounces (fluid)	Liters	
Pounds (dry)	Kilograms	
Ounces (dry)	Grams	

(continued)

Name _____ Date _____

Cooking in Metric *(continued)*

Recipe Conversions

1. If you had to make one of your recipes for the entire school, how would you know how much of each ingredient to use? Select a recipe. Figure out how much of each ingredient you would need. List the amounts in both customary and metric units.

Original Recipe	**Customary Units (for Entire School)**	**Metric Units (for Entire School)**

2. When you calculated the ingredient amounts for the recipe above, which system of measurements, customary or metric, was easier to use? Explain.

_____

_____

3. Write a problem where it is necessary to convert a recipe to a larger or smaller number of servings. Give it to another student in the class to solve.

Jell-O Jigglers™

Go to the Jell-O Jigglers recipe web site and write down the recipe. Convert the measurements to metric. Calculate how much of each ingredient you would need to serve your class. Once you have your amounts, compare your amounts with another group to see how your answers compare. If everyone in the group agrees on the recipe amounts, then make your Jell-O Jigglers—and enjoy!

Jell-O Jigglers
http://www.kraftfood.com/jell-o/world/recipeframe.html

Coin Toss

Overview:

In this activity students will conduct a simple probability experiment using a coin toss simulation on the Internet. They will then compare that with a classroom coin toss experiment.

Learning Objectives:

- Using data collected from the entire class, analyze data from the Internet coin toss simulation probability experiment.

- Compare the results of their Internet coin toss simulation with the theoretical probability for a coin toss.

- Compare the results of the theoretical Internet simulation and experimental probabilities for a coin toss.

- Make a prediction for a probability problem and verify results using the Internet.

Web Sites:

Coin Toss Simulator
http://shazam.econ.ubc.ca/flip/

Materials:

Computer with Internet access; coins or two-color counters, number depending on class size.

Suggestions:

1. This lesson is appropriate for individual students or pairs of students.

2. You may want to review the concepts of simple probability with students prior to this lesson.

3. When students are using the coin toss simulator on the Internet, they will need to select the number of coins and the number of tosses.

4. In the exercise that has students tossing the coin twenty times, you may want to vary the number of tosses depending on the level of your students, number of students, or time constraints.

5. It is important to make the distinction between theoretical and experimental probability throughout this lesson.

Selected Answers:

Answers will vary depending on results of coin tosses.

Extensions:

Vary the number of coin tosses or do another experiment with additional coins.

Coin Toss

Theoretical Probability

Let's say you are walking home from school and you notice a man walking in front of you. It just so happens that this man has 10 pennies in his pocket. It also just so happens that he has a hole in his pocket just big enough for one penny to fall out every few steps. As he walks, the first penny falls out of his pocket and rolls to a stop. You bend over to pick it up, and you notice it is heads. A few moments later, another penny falls out, and you notice it is tails. You start to wonder, "When the next penny falls out, what is the probability that it will be heads?" Explain how you would answer your question.

_____

_____

_____

You keep following the man, and by the time you get home he has lost all 10 of his pennies. Explain how many of the coins landed heads side up and how many coins landed on tails.

_____

_____

Coin Toss Simulation

1. The situation of the man losing his pennies is an example of a *theoretical* probability problem. Conduct a simulation to find the *experimental* probability of a similar problem. Go to the web site below, which simulates the toss of a coin. Flip the coin 20 times. Fill in the table with your results.

Coin Toss Simulation
http://shazam.econ.ubc.ca/flip/

INTERNET COIN TOSS SIMULATION RESULTS

Number of Heads	Number of Tails	Total Number of Flips	Probability Heads	Probability Tails

2. Combine the results from your simulation with those from the other members of your class. Fill in the table on the next page.

(continued)

Name _____ Date _____

Coin Toss *(continued)*

CLASS DATA FROM INTERNET COIN TOSS SIMULATION RESULTS

Number of Heads	Number of Tails	Total Number of Flips	Probability Heads	Probability Tails

3. Compare the results from your Internet simulation coin toss experiment with the results obtained by the class as a whole. Why are they different? Explain.

_____

_____

Coin Toss Experiments

1. Now conduct the experiment using a coin or two-color counter. Flip the coin or counter 20 times. Record your results in the table below. Then collect the results from the entire class and fill in the next table.

COIN TOSS RESULTS

Number of Heads	Number of Tails	Total Number of Flips	Probability Heads	Probability Tails

CLASS DATA FROM COIN TOSS

Number of Heads	Number of Tails	Total Number of Flips	Probability Heads	Probability Tails

2. How did the theoretical Internet simulation and actual coin toss probabilities compare with each other? Explain.

_____

_____

_____

Using the Internet to Investigate Math

Dice Roll

Overview:

In this activity students will conduct a simple probability experiment using a dice roll simulator on the Internet. They will then compare the results with a classroom dice roll experiment.

Learning Objectives:

- Conduct a simple probability experiment using a dice roll simulator on the Internet.

- Using data collected from the entire class, analyze the Internet dice roll simulation probability experiment.

- Compare the results of the Internet dice roll simulation with the theoretical probability for a die roll.

- Compare the results of the theoretical Internet simulation and experimental probabilities for a die roll.

- Make a prediction of a probability problem and verify results using the Internet.

Web Sites:

Dice roll simulator
http://www.irony.com/igroll.html

Materials:

Computer with Internet access; dice (number cubes), number varying with class size.

Suggestions:

1. This lesson is appropriate for individual students or pairs of students.

2. You may want to review the concepts of simple probability with students prior to this lesson.

3. It is important to make the distinction between theoretical and experimental probability throughout the course of this lesson.

4. When conducting the dice roll activity, you may want to use more than one die, depending on the level of your students, number of students, and time constraints.

Selected Answers:

1. 3/6; 3/6; 4/6; 4/6; 3/6; 1/6; and 0.

Extensions:

Consider having students investigate this problem. What is the probability that two people in your class have the same birthday? Compare the results to the mathematical model found at the web site below.

http://www.mste.uiuc.edu/reese/birthday/intro.html

Dice Roll

Theoretical Probability of a Dice Toss

1. Answer the questions below based on the theoretical probability of tossing a die.

   If one die is tossed once, what is the probability that the number rolled is

   even: _____

   odd: _____

   prime: _____

   less than five: _____

   greater than three: _____

   a five: _____

   a number greater than eight: _____

2. Go to the web site below and conduct the following experiment. Have the computer roll one die 20 times. Record the results of each roll in the table.

   Dice Toss Simulator
   http://www.irony.com/igroll.html

INTERNET SIMULATION DIE ROLL

Die Roll Result	1	2	3	4	5	6
Tally						
Frequency						

Combine the results from your Internet simulation with the results from the other members of your class. Fill in the table on the next page.

(continued)

Dice Roll *(continued)*

CLASS DATA FOR INTERNET SIMULATION DIE ROLL

Die Roll Results	1	2	3	4	5	6
Frequency						

3. Based on the class data for the Internet simulation probability, what is the probability of getting a number that is

   even: _____

   odd: _____

   prime: _____

   less than five: _____

   greater than three: _____

   a five: _____

   a number greater than eight: _____

4. Write a statement comparing the theoretical probability to the Internet simulated probability of your experiment.

   _____

   _____

   _____

Actual Dice Roll

   Conduct the experiment by rolling a die 20 times yourself. Record your results in the table on the next page. Collect the data from the class and record that in the next table.

(continued)

Dice Roll *(continued)*

DICE ROLL RESULTS

Die Roll Result	1	2	3	4	5	6
Tally						
Frequency						

CLASS DATA DICE ROLL RESULTS

Dice Roll Results	1	2	3	4	5	6
Frequency						

1. Based on the class data, list the experimental probability results:

    even: _____

    odd: _____

    prime: _____

    less than five: _____

    greater than three: _____

    a five: _____

    a number greater than eight: _____

2. How did the theoretical Internet simulation and die roll probabilities compare with each other? Explain.

    _____

    _____

3. Explain why gathering the class data is important.

    _____

    _____

How Many People Have Ever Lived?

Overview:

In this lesson students analyze historical population data and investigate current population information.

Learning Objectives:

- Determine appropriate intervals for graphs.
- Construct a line graph.
- Interpret and analyze the data using line graphs.
- Collect population data and use that information to determine population percentages.

Web Sites:

World Population Growth
http://www.popin.org/6billion/t01.htm

CIA Factbook
http://www.odci.gov/cia/publications/factbook/index.html

Materials:

Computer with Internet access; calculator; grid paper

Suggestions:

1. This activity works best for individual students; however, it can also be used by students working in pairs.

2. Many students need practice on how to select appropriate intervals for their graphs. You may choose to work through this portion of the activity with the whole class.

Selected Answers:

Historical Population Graph:

1. x-axis, year, y-axis, population.

2. Interval choices will vary but should be close to 25 years and 0.5 billion people.

3. Between 1990 and 2000, world population is projected to increase by 0.93 billion; however, between 1980 and 1990 actual population increased 0.85 billion.

4. 1.26×10^9, 5.3×10^9

5. Answers will vary depending upon life expectancy used in the calculation.

6. About 3 times.

Where Do You Fit in:

1. China: 1,247,000,000; India: 1,001,000,000; United States: 273,000,000; Indonesia: 216,000,000; Brazil: 172,000,000.

Extensions:

Have students graph the population data using a graphing calculator or spreadsheet.

How Many People Have Ever Lived?

People have always been fascinated with population. A lot of time, energy, and money goes into trying to figure out just how many of us there are. In this activity you will have a chance to find out how you fit into the bigger population picture.

Historical Population Graph

The web site below lists population estimates since the year "0." Use that information to construct a line graph. Before you construct the graph, answer questions 1 and 2.

World Population Growth
http://www.popin.org/6billion/t01.htm

1. Which variable, population or year, should you represent on the x-axis (horizontal axis), and which variable should you represent on the y-axis (vertical axis)?

   x-axis variable: _____

   y-axis variable: _____

2. If you plot the data only from the year 1750 forward, what would be appropriate intervals for the two variables?

   x-axis interval: _____

   y-axis interval: _____

   Use a piece of grid paper to construct a line graph. Use data only from the year 1750 forward. When you are finished, answer the questions that follow.

3. During which 10-year period did the population increase the most?

   _____

4. Write the population for the years 1850 and 1990 in scientific notation.

   _____

   _____

5. Estimate how many people have been born since 1750.

   _____

(continued)

         Using the Internet to Investigate Math

How Many People Have Ever Lived? *(continued)*

6. How many times since 1750 has the world population doubled?

_____

Where Do You Fit In?

Use the web page below to help you answer the following questions about population.

CIA Factbook
http://www.odci.gov/cia/publications/factbook/index.html

1. Look up the population of the United States, China, India, Indonesia, and Brazil. Round each country's population to the nearest 10 million, then list each population in the table. Then write it in scientific notation.

WORLD POPULATION

Country	Population (Rounded to Nearest 10 Million)	Population in Scientific Notation	Percent of Total World's Population	Decimal Equivalent	Fraction Equivalent
United States					
China					
India					
Indonesia					
Brazil					

2. Calculate each country's share of the world population. Enter that amount into the table. Then figure out the decimal and fraction equivalents and enter those amounts in the table.

3. What percentage of the United States population does your class comprise?

_____

Batter Up!

Overview:

In this lesson students act as sports agents for major league baseball players. As agents, they will learn how to select statistical criteria and use that information to make comparisons and substantiate salaries for the players.

Learning Objectives:

- Select criteria for evaluation.
- Analyze and interpret data.
- Represent data in meaningful ways.

Web Sites:

ESPN Baseball Players Index
http://espn.go.com/mlb/profiles/index.html

ESPN Baseball Statistics
http://espn.go.com/mlb/statistics/index.html

Materials:

Computer with Internet access; calculator; computer with word processing software

Suggestions:

1. This activity can be done by individual students, in pairs, or in small groups.

2. As a warm-up to the lesson, ask students what they think are the most important criteria in judging a baseball player's performance.

3. If you are using this lesson late in the baseball season, you may choose to use the current year's statistics.

4. In the first table, some students may confuse the fact that a lower score is better than a higher score.

5. In the second table, some students may confuse the fact that a higher score is better than a lower score.

6. For the second table, if a criterion is represented as a decimal, such as batting average, have students convert that number to a whole number.

Selected Answers:

Answers will vary depending upon players chosen.

Extensions:

1. This activity can be adapted to work with almost any sport.

2. Have students use a word processor to write their letters to the team owners.

Batter Up!

Suppose you are a sports agent who represents five major league baseball players. It seems that it's time to negotiate new contracts for the players you represent. To make the best deal possible, you have to prove to the owner of the team that the players you represent are worth what you are asking. One way to do that would be to gather data (evidence) that demonstrates their worth and use that information in a meaningful and convincing way. Since the owner has limited math skills, you will have to be careful to organize your data in a way that clearly makes your point. Good luck and good negotiating.

Table 1: Criteria Ranking

Who is the best hitter in baseball? Baseball historians, writers, and fans have argued for decades about that. Now it's your chance to prove them all wrong. Choose five players from the web site below and write their names in the first column of Table 1. These will be the players you represent. You will have to rank these five players in order from best to worst according to their hitting ability. This will help you decide how much to ask for in each player's contract. In other words, the best hitter in the group should receive the highest pay.

ESPN Baseball Players Index
http://espn.go.com/mlb/profiles/index.html

1. Having the highest batting average or hitting the most home runs doesn't necessarily mean that you are the best hitter. It is simply one way to measure or one criterion that is used to decide. If you are familiar with baseball, you know that many statistics can be used to evaluate hitters. For this activity you will evaluate hitters based on their Batting Average, Runs Batted In (RBI), Home Runs, and Runs Scored. To find out more about how statistics are used in baseball, visit the web site below.

ESPN Baseball Statistics
http://espn.go.com/mlb/statistics/index.html

(continued)

Batter Up! *(continued)*

TABLE 1: CRITERIA RANKING

Player's Name	Batting Average	Rank	Home Runs	Rank	RBI	Rank	Runs Scored	Rank	Total Points
1.									
2.									
3.									
4.									
5.									

TABLE 2: WEIGHTED SCORES

Player's Name	Batting Average	Weighted Score	Home Runs	Weighted Score	RBI	Weighted Score	Runs Scored	Weighted Score	Total Weighted Score
1.									
2.									
3.									
4.									
5.									

(continued)

Batter Up! *(continued)*

2. Now go the the web site below. Look up each of the four statistics from last year for each player you represent. List the amounts for each category in Table 1. Leave the column labeled "rank" blank until you have filled in all the categories.

   ESPN Baseball Statistics
   http://espn.go.com/mlb/statistics/index.html

3. After you have filled in the amounts, rank each player by criteria using a 5-point scale, with a 1 being the best in the group and a 5 being the worst.

4. When you finish assigning points to each category, total the points. List that amount in the last column of Table 1.

Table 2: Weighted Scores

1. The ranking system you used to fill in Table 1 assumed that all four of your criteria are equally important. Look over the four statistics. Rank them in order of importance from most important to least important. For instance, if the criteria you are using are home runs, on-base percentage, RBI, and at bats, then you might decide that home runs are most important and should count for 40%, RBI are next most important and should count for 30%, and so on. Carefully assess the importance of each criterion and assign a percent value to it. Finish the table by converting the percentages to decimals. As a check, make sure your percentages add up to 100, and decimals to 1.00.

Criteria	Batting Average	Home Runs	RBI	Runs Scored	Total
Percent Assigned					100
Decimal Equivalent					1.00

2. Now fill out Table 2. First, list the players' names in column 1, and fill in the data for each of the four criteria. Perform the necessary calculations. Then enter decimal weighting. Next, total each player's score and enter that amount in the table.

(continued)

Batter Up! *(continued)*

Analyze Your Findings

1. Using the information from both tables, list each player's rankings and weighted scores in the table below. Remember, for Table 1 the top score is the lowest amount, and for Table 2 the top score is the highest amount.

Table 1 Ranking	Table 2 Ranking
1.	1.
2.	2.
3.	3.
4.	4.
5.	5.

2. Predict how a player's score would change if you added an additional statistical category.

   _____

   _____

   _____

3. How were the results of Table 1 and Table 2 similar? How were they different? Explain.

   _____

   _____

   _____

Present Your Case

Write a letter to the owner of a team convincing him or her that your client is worth what you are asking. As part of your letter, use the information from the tables in support of your position.

Chill Out

Overview:

In this year-long activity students gather weather data from cities across the United States to calculate wind chill index.

Learning Objectives:

- Select cities by climate.
- Collect weather data over a period of time.
- Use the Internet to calculate the wind chill index for their cities.
- Calculate the average wind chill index for each month for which they collect data.
- Analyze, interpret, and make predictions using their data.

Web Sites:

National Geographic Map of United States
http://www.plasma.nationalgeographic.com/mapmachine/facts_fs.html

Weather by State
http://weather.yahoo.com/regional/US.html

Wind Chill Calculator
http://water.dnr.state.sc.us/cgi-bin/sercc/windchill.cgi

Wind Chill Chart
http://asd.planetarium.org/weather/Wind-chill-index.html

Materials:

Computer with Internet access; calculator; graphing paper

Suggestions:

1. This activity can be done individually, in pairs, or by small groups.

2. To conduct the activity as described on the handout, begin the activity at the beginning of the school year so that students can collect data for nine months.

3. This investigation can be modified in a number of different ways, depending upon your needs. You can shorten the period of data collection, or you can have students collect data more frequently during a given month. You may choose to include more cities or cities outside the United States.

4. If your school has a weather observation station, you can also have students collect data at school.

Selected Answers:

Answers will vary depending upon which cities are selected.

Extensions:

1. The data can be used to construct graphs using a graphing calculator or spreadsheet software. Have students construct scatter-plots exploring the relationship between the temperature and wind speed.

2. Convert temperatures to degrees Celsius.

Chill Out

Have you ever heard a weather forecast go something like this: "The low temperature will be 38 degrees, but it will feel like 25 degrees"? What is it that makes it feel that much colder? That's right—the wind makes it feel cooler. Temperature and wind are measured using a wind chill index. Explore the relationship between temperature and wind by working through the investigation below.

Select Cities to Study

Use the web site below to select cities from which to gather weather data. Choose five cities in cooler climates to analyze wind chill data. Once you have selected your cities, enter them in the appropriate section of the Wind Chill Index Table.

National Geographic Map of United States
http://www.plasma.nationalgeographic.com/mapmachine/facts_fs.html

Collect Weather Data

Over the course of the next nine months, visit the web site below once a month to collect the temperatures and wind speeds for the cities. Enter the weather data in the table; however, leave the Wind Chill Index sections blank for now.

Weather by State
http://weather.yahoo.com/regional/US.html
(Follow the link to your city's state, and then locate the city in that state.)

Wind Chill Index

After you have recorded the temperatures and wind speeds for each cold climate city, go to the web site below and calculate the wind chill indexes. At the web site, enter the temperature and wind speed for each month. Then press the "calculate" button. Enter the results in the table on the Wind Chill Index row.

Wind Chill Calculator
http://water.dnr.state.sc.us/cgi-bin/sercc/windchill.cgi

Analyze the Data

Once you have calculated the wind chill index for each city during a given month, use that information to determine the average wind chill index for all five cities during that month. Enter the monthly average at the bottom of the table. After you have recorded the wind chill indexes for all nine months, use that information to calculate the average wind chill index for each individual city for the nine-month period.

(continued)

Chill Out (continued)

What Is the Relationship?

One way to examine data is by constructing a graph. On a separate sheet of paper, build a graph comparing the average wind chill indexes for the cities in a given month. When you have finished constructing the graph, answer the following questions.

1. Describe the relationship between the average wind chill index and the months of the year.

   _____

   _____

   _____

2. Predict what the average wind chill index would be in July. Explain how you made your prediction.

   _____

   _____

   _____

3. How would the average wind chill index change if you combined the data for all the cities?

   _____

   _____

   _____

4. Hypothesize about a general rule or write a formula for determining the wind chill index if you know the temperature and wind speed. Experiment with your hypothesis and check your conclusions using the wind chill index chart web site found below.

   Wind Chill Chart
   http://asd.planetarium.org/weather/Wind-chill-index.html

   _____

   _____

   _____

(continued)

Name _____   Date _____

Chill Out *(continued)*

WIND CHILL INDEX TABLE

	Sep.	Oct.	Nov.	Dec.	Jan.	Feb.	Mar.	Apr.	May	

City Name: _____

Day										
Air Temp (F)										
Wind Speed (mph)										Avg
Wind Chill Index										

City Name: _____

Day										
Air Temp (F)										
Wind Speed (mph)										Avg
Wind Chill Index										

City Name: _____

Day										
Air Temp (F)										
Wind Speed (mph)										Avg
Wind Chill Index										

City Name: _____

Day										
Air Temp (F)										
Wind Speed (mph)										Avg
Wind Chill Index										

City Name: _____

Day										
Air Temp (F)										
Wind Speed (mph)										Avg
Wind Chill Index										

	Sep.	Oct.	Nov.	Dec.	Jan.	Feb.	Mar.	Apr.	May
Monthly Average									

The Heat Is On

Overview:

In this year-long activity students gather weather data from cities across the United States to calculate the heat index.

Learning Objectives:

- Select cities by climate.
- Collect weather data over a period of time.
- Use the Internet to calculate the heat index for cities.
- Calculate the average heat index for each month for which they collect data.
- Analyze, interpret, and make predictions using data.

Web Sites:

National Geographic Map of United States
http://www.plasma.nationalgeographic.com/mapmachine/facts_fs.html

Weather by State
http://weather.yahoo.com/regional/US.html

Heat Index Calculator
http://nwselp.epcc.edu/elp/heatindex.html

Heat Index Chart
http://leav-www.army.mil/weather/Heatindx.htm

Materials:

Computer with Internet access; calculator; graphing paper

Suggestions:

1. This activity can be done individually, in pairs, or by small groups.

2. To conduct the activity as described on the handout, begin the activity at the beginning of the school year so that students can collect data for nine months.

3. This investigation can be modified in a number of different ways, depending upon your needs. You can shorten the period of data collection, or you can have students collect data more frequently during a given month. You may choose to include more cities or cities outside the United States.

4. If your school has a weather observation station, you can also have students collect data at school.

Selected Answers:

Answers will vary depending upon which cities are selected.

Extensions:

1. The data can be used to construct graphs using a graphing calculator or spreadsheet software. Have students construct scatter-plots exploring the relationship between the temperature and relative humidity.

2. Convert temperatures to degrees Celsius.

The Heat Is On

Have you ever heard a weather forecast go something like this: "The high temperature will be 92 degrees, but it will feel like 112 degrees?" What is it that makes it feel that much hotter? It's the humidity—the amount of moisture there is in the air. Temperature and humidity are measured using a heat index. Explore the relationship between temperature and humidity by working through the investigation below.

Select Cities to Study

Use the web site below to select cities from which to gather weather data. Choose five cities in warmer climates to analyze heat index data. Once you have selected your cities, enter them in the appropriate section of the Heat Index Table.

National Geographic Map of United States
http://www.plasma.nationalgeographic.com/mapmachine/facts_fs.html

Collect Weather Data

Over the course of the next nine months, visit the web site below once a month. Collect the temperatures and relative humidities for the cities. Enter the weather data in the table; however, leave the Heat Index sections blank for now.

Weather by State
http://weather.yahoo.com/regional/US.html
(Follow the link to your city's state, and then locate the city in that state.)

Heat Index

After you have recorded the temperatures and relative humidities for each city, go to the web site below and calculate the heat indexes. At the web site, enter the temperature and relative humidity for each month and press the "calculate it" button. Enter the results in the table in the row labeled Heat Index.

Heat Index Calculator
http://nwselp.epcc.edu/elp/heatindex.html

Analyze the Data

Once you have calculated the heat index for each city during a given month, use that information to determine the average heat index for all five cities during that month. Enter the monthly average at the bottom of the table. After you have recorded the heat indexes for all nine months, use that information to calculate the average heat index for each individual city for the nine-month period.

(continued)

The Heat Is On

What Is the Relationship?

One way to examine data is by constructing a graph. On a separate sheet of paper, construct a graph comparing the average heat indexes for the cities in a given month. When you have finished constructing the graph, answer the following questions.

1. Describe the relationship between the average heat index and the months of the year.

   _____

   _____

   _____

2. Predict what the average heat index would be in August. Explain how you made your prediction.

   _____

   _____

   _____

3. How would the average heat indexes change if you combined the data for all the cities?

   _____

   _____

   _____

4. Hypothesize about a general rule or write a formula for determining the heat index if you know the temperature and relative humidity. Experiment with your hypothesis and check your conclusions using the heat index table web site found below.

   Heat Index Chart
   http://leav-www.army.mil/weather/Heatindx.htm

   _____

   _____

   _____

(continued)

The Heat Is On *(continued)*

HEAT INDEX TABLE

	Sep.	Oct.	Nov.	Dec.	Jan.	Feb.	Mar.	Apr.	May	

City Name: _____

Day										
Air Temp (F)										
Relative Humidity										Avg
Heat Index										

City Name: _____

Day										
Air Temp (F)										
Relative Humidity										Avg
Heat Index										

City Name: _____

Day										
Air Temp (F)										
Relative Humidity										Avg
Heat Index										

City Name: _____

Day										
Air Temp (F)										
Relative Humidity										Avg
Heat Index										

City Name: _____

Day										
Air Temp (F)										
Relative Humidity										Avg
Heat Index										

	Sep.	Oct.	Nov.	Dec.	Jan.	Feb.	Mar.	Apr.	May
Monthly Average									

Using the Internet to Investigate Math

General Scoring Rubric

The general scoring rubric below shows some of the factors that might be considered when scoring the students' work.

4 Exemplary Response

Student's response clearly shows an in-depth and thorough understanding of the activity's mathematical concepts and content. Written explanations are clear, concise, and insightful. Contains few, if any, computational errors, and student has made appropriate use of mathematical symbols and terms. Supporting graphs, tables, charts, and diagrams are accurate and contain essential elements. A high level of mathematical thinking is evident. Overall, the response exceeds expectations.

3 Competent Response

Student's response shows a good understanding of the activity's mathematical concepts and content. Written explanations are reasonably clear and thoughtful. Contains minor computational errors, and in most cases mathematical symbols and terms have been used appropriately. Supporting graphs, tables, charts, and diagrams contain small errors in accuracy. Overall, the response is solid.

2 Satisfactory Response

Student's response shows some understanding of the activity's mathematical concepts and content. Written explanations are attempted but may be incomplete or unclear. Contains many computational errors, and mathematical symbols and terms are misused. Supporting graphs, tables, charts, and diagrams contain significant errors in accuracy and detail. Overall, the response is below expectations.

1 Unsatisfactory Response

Student's response shows little or no understanding of the activity's mathematical concepts and content. Written explanations are incoherent. Contains major computational errors, and mathematical symbols and terms are used incorrectly most of the time. Supporting graphs, tables, charts, and diagrams are inaccurate and may misrepresent the problem. Overall, the response is unacceptable.

0 No Attempt

Student makes no attempt.

Math Web Sites

The comprehensive mathematics web sites listed below contain valuable information and can be used as starting points for further exploration of the Internet.

The Math Forum Home Page
http://forum.swarthmore.edu/

The Math Forum is the most comprehensive math site on the Internet. Highlights include the following: "Ask Dr. Math," "Problem of the Week," and numerous other resources. Begin your exploration here.

Eisenhower National Clearinghouse for Mathematics and Science Education
http://www.enc.org/

The Eisenhower National Clearinghouse for Mathematics and Science Education (ENC) provides K-12 teachers with a central source of information on mathematics and science curriculum materials.

National Council of Teachers of Mathematics' Web Site
http://www.nctm.org/

Stay current with what's happening in math education by visiting NCTM's web site.

The ERIC Clearinghouse for Science, Mathematics, and Environmental Education
http://www.ericse.org/

ERIC/CSMEE produces digests and bulletins that summarize current issues in mathematics education. These are excellent resources for conducting research. The web site also has comprehensive links to lessons, organizations, announcements, and journals.

Share Your Bright Ideas with Us!

We want to hear from you! Your valuable comments and suggestions will help us meet your current and future classroom needs.

Your name_____Date_____

School name_____Phone_____

School address_____

Grade level taught_____Subject area(s) taught_____Average class size_____

Where did you purchase this publication?_____

Was your salesperson knowledgeable about this product?   Yes_____   No_____

What monies were used to purchase this product?

____School supplemental budget   ____Federal/state funding   ____Personal

Please "grade" this Walch publication according to the following criteria:

Quality of service you received when purchasing .... A   B   C   D   F
Ease of use.. A   B   C   D   F
Quality of content.. A   B   C   D   F
Page layout .... A   B   C   D   F
Organization of material .... A   B   C   D   F
Suitability for grade level .... A   B   C   D   F
Instructional value... A   B   C   D   F

COMMENTS:_____

_____

What specific supplemental materials would help you meet your current—or future—instructional needs?

_____

Have you used other Walch publications? If so, which ones?_____

May we use your comments in upcoming communications?   ____Yes   ____No

Please **FAX** this completed form to **207-772-3105**, or mail it to:

Product Development, J. Weston Walch, Publisher, P.O. Box 658, Portland, ME 04104-0658

We will send you a **FREE GIFT** as our way of thanking you for your feedback.   **THANK YOU!**